Joan Cass

The Significance of Children's Play

B. T. Batsford Ltd London

First published 1971
© Joan Cass 1971
Reprinted 1972
3rd impression, 1st limp edition 1977

Printed in Great Britain by
Billing & Sons Ltd.,
Guildford, London and Worcester
for the publishers B. T. Batsford Ltd
4 Fitzhardinge Street, London W1H 0AH

ISBN 0 7134 0689 5

Remembering all the children at
The Edith Kerrison Nursery School, West Ham
from whom I learnt so much and
enjoyed so wholeheartedly

Dedicated to Diana Rosemary Cass-Beggs,
my eldest niece,
with love and affection

Contents

6   *Contents*

III   *Where children play*

Safety in toys; play for a sick child; suggested play
materials for young children; firms which supply
play materials and equipment; books; periodicals
concerned with children's books

Preface

One's own experiences are always vitally important in whatever one is writing about and in this book on the play of young children I have drawn extensively on my own knowledge and experience over a long period with children from two to eight.

When I was head of a large nursery school I watched and shared the spontaneous play of the under fives from a great variety of different homes and backgrounds and I am especially grateful for all that the children taught me, for the pleasure and enjoyment of it all that made the learning so delightful, and for the contacts I have had with the children of relatives and friends as I have watched them grow from babyhood into teenagers and adults.

I was fortunate, too, in having a childhood which was full of happy, satisfying play in a secure and loving setting on which I can look back with deep appreciation.

Apart from all the children, I would especially like to thank a number of friends who have read this book in manuscript and have made useful and valuable suggestions: Miss Kathleen Lade, Mr and Mrs Richards, and Mrs Edna O'Shaughnessy, whose comments were so apt, Miss Cynthia Doubtfire for assistance with the bibliography and some of the autobiographical quotations, Mrs Nora Williams and Mrs Cynthia James for many of the observations on the children's play from their unpublished theses, Mr Peter Ibbotson for many final corrections in the text and Mr David Platt for reading the proofs so adequately for me.

I hope that the book may be of some use to teachers, students, houseparents and parents, in fact to anyone who has contacts with children and can in some way enrich and enhance their play life. I have tried to make it readable.

The friends and children who have helped me so much cannot of course be blamed for any of my errors or opinions.

PART ONE

Why children play

When Childher Plays

Now the beauty of the thing when childher plays is
The terrible wonderful length the days is.
Up you jumps, and out in the sun,
And you fancy the day will never be done;
And you're chasin' the bum bees hummin' so cross
In the hot sweet air among the goss,
Or gath'rin' bluebells, or lookin' for eggs,
Or peltin' the ducks with their yalla legs,
Or a climbin' and nearly breakin' your skulls,
Or a shoutin' for divilment after the gulls,
Or a thinkin' of nothin' but down at the tide,
Singin' out for the happy you feel inside.
And when you look back it's all a puff,
Happy and over and short enough.

T. E. BROWN

1

What is play?

Why do children play? Is it just a simple, harmless way of passing the time, of keeping them happily employed so that they do not interfere unduly with the important business of adult living? Has play any real significance for them and would it not be better to see that they were employed in other more useful and productive pursuits?

In an age when the speed and intensity of living in a highly-organized and complex society often makes enormous demands on both adults and boys and girls, should we not prepare children as soon as possible for the kind of life experiences they are going to meet, when intellectual skills are going to be so necessary and important to them in order that they may be equipped in the best possible way to cope with the problems and difficulties they will have to face in the world of today?

Most of us are aware that if a child is to have the right start in life, apart from his obvious need to be fed, clothed and sheltered, he must have the generous love and attention that a warm and understanding mother, or mother substitute, can provide.

He needs to belong somewhere and to have his place in a family or extended family where he will be accepted and wanted for himself and where his personality will be able to develop in a secure and stable environment.

There is ample research available which shows the effects which a broken home and parental rejection, separation and severe instability can have on a young child's healthy development; even brief separation from home and family can have harmful results for many children.

There have been numerous studies to this effect. John Bowlby's[1] well-known work, *Maternal Care and Mental Health*, the work of Anna Freud and Dorothy Burlingham[2] during the late war, and the most recent films of James Robertson[3] show how a brief withdrawal of the mother, even when good foster home care is available, induces unhappy and undesirable reactions in young children. Even young Rhesus monkeys separated from their mothers show by their behaviour that they, too, need a caring relationship in their early months of life.

In present day society higher standards of living, valuable and necessary as they are, often mean that young children grow up in a world singularly unsuited to their needs. Material assets have become important and good furniture, neat gardens, numerous possessions and elegant schools are all an indication that a prosperous and civilized nation exists. No one would, for one moment, grudge human beings their right to these things but children often find themselves restricted, inhibited and confined with few outlets for their energetic bodies, busy fingers, inquisitive minds and spontaneous feelings. Space is at a premium, behaviour must be circumspect and noise is an anathema; in fact, real lively, inventive and creative play has become almost impossible.

Yet play is as necessary and important to a child as the food he eats, for it is the very breath of life to him, the reason for his existence and his assurance of immortality.

It is an activity which is concerned with the whole of his being, not with just one small part of him, and to deny him the right to play is to deny him the right to live and grow. It is as if one imprisoned him in an ivory tower or a golden cage. Through the bars he might be able to look out on what was happening, safe from danger and disaster, but of what use would this enforced security be to him cut off from the real world of people and things?

Society has been slow to recognize or provide adequately for children's play needs. Perhaps because play has no end results which can be considered as materially useful or productive it has been lightly dismissed or frowned upon. For the very spirit of play is that it is an end in itself, there is no compulsion about it, it can be laid aside at will for it is its own final justification. The fact that children do produce beautiful paintings and models, or dance, act and build when they are playing does not affect the real issue that these activities are spontaneously chosen and can be discarded at will.

Children do enjoy their play enormously and this too is sometimes slightly suspect, particularly if what they are doing brings them into conflict with the adult world, for there is a feeling abroad that if play, as it sometimes appears to be, is a form of self-indulgence, then we are surely spoiling children if we do not inhibit and restrict these activities.

Yet play uses every ounce of a child's energy. It encourages his imagination. It develops skills of both body and mind. It brings about understanding, warmth, and sympathy towards others.

How to compete, how to take hard knocks, how to win gracefully; when to assert oneself and when to forget self-interest are all learned through play. Perseverance, how to struggle through to a desired end, is as much a part of play as it is of work.

Play offers healing for hurts and sadness. It breaks down tension and releases pent-up urges towards self-expression. Play is the working partner of growth, for activity is as vital to growth as food and sleep.

The far-reaching significance of children's play has only lately been understood. Unless the deep-lying impulses satisfied by play are allowed to express themselves in childhood, adult life suffers.

Some men and women are never able to take part freely in the life around them; they are stiff and lonely because they don't know how to mix with others. They cannot lose themselves in spontaneous fun.

Somehow or other their urges towards expression in play were denied the chance to come to the surface in childhood.[4]

Because play is so universal an activity it obviously could not go completely unnoticed and unrecognized and there have been many theories to explain and define play.

The Greek philosophers Plato and Aristotle, Comenius in the seventeenth century, Rousseau, Pestalozzi, and Froebel in the early eighteenth and nineteenth centuries were aware that play had a definite purpose, but they made little attempt to explain it in developmental terms although they stressed its value.

The English philosopher Herbert Spencer in his book *Principles of Psychology* elaborated the theory, which in fact he originally obtained from the writings of the poet and philosopher Friedrich von Schiller, that play was a manifestation of surplus energy.

Preyer, a German physiologist, and Stanley Hall, an American professor, both made careful and systematic observations of actual children and Stanley Hall developed the recapitulation theory whereby children relive, as it were, in their play the history of the human race from the protozoa to present-day man. Karl Groos, a German professor, watching animals at play saw their activities, and those of children too, as a practice ground for the skills needed in adult life. Other theories suggested that play restored the individual who was physically and mentally tired, that play acted as a safety valve for pent-up feelings or as a means of self-expression.

Freud was concerned with the relationship between imaginative play and emotion and in his classic description of the 18-month-old baby whom he observed letting down a cotton reel from his cot, tied on a piece of string, he describes how it appeared to him that the infant was able to compensate himself in fantasy for the absence of his beloved mother. In his play he was able symbolically to let his mother go for he knew, through his experience, that eventually she was going to return.

Piaget's theory of play is closely bound up with his account of the growth of intelligence : 'He postulates two processes which he believes to be fundamental to all organic development; assimilation and accommodation. . . . The two processes are complementary and involve each other. Piaget has no need to assume a special impulse to play, since he regards it as an aspect of assimilation. . . . His theory implies that intellectual development proceeds in a sequence which may be accelerated or retarded but cannot itself be changed by experience.'[5]

In his book, *Play, Dreams and Imitation in Childhood*,[6] he bases his material on the detailed case histories of his three children from birth through early childhood and gives a much more detailed picture of how play appears to him.

Melanie Klein developed the spontaneous play with young

children in the psychoanalytic situation as a means of both discovering and helping them to solve their problems and by interpreting the wishes, fears, anxieties and conflicts which their play revealed.

Susan Isaacs in her two books, *Intellectual Growth in Young Children* and *Social Development in Young Children*,[7] based on records of the work carried on at the Malting House School in Cambridge from October 1924 to Christmas 1927, shows the value of children's play in spontaneous activity in a rich and challenging environment with skilled adults at hand. In writing of the function of play she says, 'The life of infancy and earliest childhood is largely dominated by the primary mechanisms of introjection and projection. The influence of displacement is continually at work from the earliest days leading to the first sublimation of primitive phantasies in the earliest forms of play. The chief function of play in these early years is the active dramatization of the inner world of phantasy as a means of maintaining psychic equilibrium. In his play activities the child externalizes and works out to some measure of harmony all the different trends of his internal psychic life. In turn he gives external form and expression now to the parent, now to the child within himself, and to each of the different aspects of his real parents, as he apprehends them at different levels of his own development, through his own wishes and impulses.'[8]

Erikson, in discussing play, suggests some of the differences between child and adult play.

When man plays [he says] he must intermingle with things and people in a similarly uninvolved and light fashion. He must do something which he has chosen to do without being compelled by urgent interests or impelled by strong passions; he must feel entertained and free of any fear or hope of serious consequences. He is on vacation from social and economic reality— or, as is most commonly emphasized, he does not work. . . . 'Man is perfectly human only when he plays', said Schiller. Thus play is a borderline phenomenon to a number of human activities and, in its own playful way, it tries to elude definition.

It is true that even the most strenuous and dangerous play is by definition not work; it does not produce commodities.

Where it does, it 'goes professional'. But this fact from the start, makes the comparison of adult and child's play somewhat senseless; for the adult is a commodity-producing and commodity-exchanging being, where as a child he is only preparing to become one. To the working adult, play is recreation. It permits a periodical stepping out from those forms of defined limitations which are his social reality.[9]

We know that young animals need to play, and this need appears to be more varied and frequent among the higher mammals and is probably linked with their greater ability to learn. Nothing can be more destructive than boredom. Confined in a zoo, if there is nothing in the environment to explore, animals in sheer desperation and frustration may mutilate themselves, destroy their young, rock backwards and forwards or pace their cages endlessly. They need something to do.

The exploratory behaviour which occurs in young animals, however, is to be found to an extreme extent in man and Dr Morris in his book *The Naked Ape* suggests that this behaviour in man 'has become emancipated as a distinct and separate drive. Its function is to provide us with a subtle and complex awareness of the world around and of our own capacities in relation to it. Children in their play investigate the unfamiliar until it becomes known. Repeat and vary it in as many ways as possible selecting the most satisfying at the expense of the others, combining and recombining these variations, one with another for their own sake.'[10] We can deny children opportunities to use these exploratory impulses if we deny or curtail their play, and there is at the moment a suggestion that too much emphasis is being put on a child's need and wish to play. The pressure-cooker approach, America's latest gimmick in which four-year-old pre-school children are drilled in Arithmetic, Language and Reading and where play is considered too time-consuming and superfluous to indulge in, could have disastrous effects.

In our anxiety to push children on it is only too easy to forget that each stage of development needs to be lived fully for its own sake. Children will never have their childhood again. If we take it away from them now, it is gone for ever.

2
Growth tasks

When I was a child I spake as a child, I understood as a child, I thought as a child.

PAUL, *First Epistle to the Corinthians*

Development in any individual involves a series of growth tasks that have to be accomplished and life presents these tasks to all of us. Each one with its logical series of sequences is built on the preceding one, and this emphasizes and underlines the importance of the early years. Early patterns of behaviour in children do not suddenly appear out of the blue; each one is built on subsequent patterns and the successful resolution of each stage will obviously affect the ones that follow.

The baby comes into the world from the warm security of the womb to face what must often appear to be a cold indifferent world. None of us can remember unaided his very early years: they are 'memories in feeling', as Melanie Klein has put it, and it is extremely difficult even to imagine a moment when we had no language at all at our disposal.

The baby has no words and no sense of time. He goes to sleep, he wakes, he feels hungry and cold and his mother with her warmth, touch and smell, the good food she provides and the way she gives it is, at first, the whole of life; to him nothing else exists.

Obviously life must feel both good and bad; good if he is warmed and fed, bad if he is hungry and cold. At first he does not think of himself and his mother as separate identities. He absorbs her (i.e. he introjects her) into himself with the good food she gives him and so identifies himself completely with her.

As well as this safe, inside world which one might almost envisage as a circle containing both mother and child, the baby feels that there must be a bad mother as well as the good one, the being that leaves him hungry and unsatisfied, cold and lonely, and so he is faced with these early feelings, primitive and intense, of both love and hate.

One can well imagine how the infant who is continually frustrated and left to cry hopelessly will gradually come to believe that the world is a hostile and fearful place dominated by hate. On the other hand the secure and satisfied baby will tend to feel that love is the predominant factor in his existence. Frustration is, of course, part of the pattern and challenge of life which all children have to face and which can act as a useful driving and growing point provided that it is within the ability of the individual to manage; all children need parents or substitute parents with whom they can experience the whole gamut of emotional responses, from warm affection to exasperation and anger. One must remember, however, that the tiny baby is dependent and helpless : he can only scream in fury and pain; and because he sees no further than the actual moment of desolation, frustration is much more damaging and harmful.

By the time a baby is a few months old he has made a very personal attachment to his mother and if he is separated from her he reacts with misery and despair. He is slowly becoming aware of himself as separate from her and is beginning to see people as whole beings rather than as unconnected manifestations that appear before him out of eternity to feed, hold and change him.

The actual presence of a young child's mother or mother substitute in his day-to-day life is vitally important. The toddler is so often with his mother, actually around her feet in the kitchen or living-room, that there is constant communication between the two.

Even when he becomes absorbed in his own affairs, playing happily with whatever he finds or has been given, if he suddenly misses her ample and enveloping care he can rush frantically to find her.

One has only to watch a group of young children under two— five or six of them, or even more, together in a residential establishment where staff changes often mean that the children have no one really permanent to whom they can become attached —to see the devastating effects on their growth and behaviour. Such children find it difficult to develop the normal skills of childhood because they cannot become absorbed in satisfying and healing play. Life for them has become a fight for emotional existence. They must, at all costs, have the notice and attention of an adult from whom they feel they may gain a little of the love and security they so badly need. So they grab, fight, push, scream, cry, and whine; notice from anyone is better than nothing.

Some children may decide, unconsciously, that all they can do is to withdraw from this unequal battle into rocking, sucking, masturbating or head-banging, a world of emptiness where relationships with adults and other children have become almost impossible.

Even an unsatisfactory mother has something unique to give her baby, and life and its tasks are going to prove even more hazardous for the child who is unwanted and rejected.

However the majority of children are born into a more or less stable family, and although there is no set of rules, no actual ground plan which if followed meticulously will produce the perfect child, the whole emotional climate of the home needs to be one that can meet the personal needs of the individual child as and when they arise.

Each position in the family presents its own particular difficulties and anxieties; each sex has its own special needs and problems of adjustment.

In the early years children tend to establish an object love towards parents of the opposite sex. The small boy becomes deeply attached to his mother and determines to marry her when he grows up. The same kind of relationship is felt by the small girl for her father whom she also plans to marry in due course. These feelings are normal and most children gradually become aware of the impossibility of these wishes. The small boy then begins to see his father, not so much as a rival but as a hero, someone with whom he can identify, who is clever, brave and manly. The small girl realizes that her mother is to be admired and copied and that in growing up to be like her she too will be able to have babies and a man of her own. If these problems of relationship are not satisfactorily resolved during the early years a boy or girl can grow up unconsciously too emotionally orientated and tied to the parents of the same or the opposite sex (tied to mother's apron strings, father's prop and darling) and can find the achieving of a mature relationship in marriage difficult, for each expects and continually demands a mother or father figure, rather than a wife or husband, in his mate.

The harsh and intolerant parent, of course, whether father or mother, will tend to arouse in a child to a much greater degree the angry, hostile elements which are part of the love/hate relationship. Children feel that here is a tyrant, whether father or mother, against whom it is essential to rebel. So the loving side of their feelings, which in satisfying relationships is the most important, tends to be swamped and crushed, often colouring the whole of adult life. Jealousy and envy between siblings is again a feature of the family, and children have to learn to manage these feelings. Not only do they see in the new arrival a threat to their place in the family, but there is also always the fear that this rival will continue to remain the best loved, the cleverest, the one who gets the most attention and receives the most gifts. Not only must parents be shared but toys, outings, festivals, food are no longer there just for the child alone.

Often boys or girls will hide their jealous feelings, knowing that if they pinch or hit this strange, helpless creature they would so like to destroy, mother or father will be angry and they may be punished; that is, they will lose love. So on the surface they appear kind, affectionate, gentle and generous even if they are seething with rage within themselves.

Fairly soon in the learning process young children are expected to become what might be called toilet-trained; that is, they must no longer wet and soil themselves indiscriminately wherever they happen to be.

This is a complex skill to master and there is often a good deal of stress and strain and love and hate associated with it. Society demands control and parents are angry and ashamed of their children who do not conform to the accepted social pattern. To please his mother, if she is loving and understanding and does not demand this skill too early, a child will try and go along with her training. If, however, she has been strict and exacting, punishing and angry, he may unconsciously get his own back on her by continuing to wet and soil during his pre-school years and even longer.

Many older children continue to wet their beds for a variety of reasons : separation from home and the insecurity this brings, an unconscious act of aggression against parents who have in some way failed the child, a fear and a refusal to grow up, a desire to hold onto baby pleasures and satisfactions.

Yet no child really wants his mother to abdicate on his toilet-training and leave him to struggle on alone to be clean without her loving support and understanding. A child's excreta can some-times appear to him, not only as something pleasurable but also as something bad and dangerous which may harm him. So he wants to be able to control his faeces and urine and not to be, as it were, at their mercy.

This means that if there is a loving relationship between a child and his mother he will want to try to cooperate with her and to become the clean, good child she wishes to have.

As children begin to develop as individuals gradually their ideas of right and wrong and of good and bad behaviour are understood in relation to the adults who love and care for them. It is as if children had their parents or those in authority over them inside themselves acting as their conscience or super-ego. The child with angry, intolerant, cruel and unaccepting parents builds, as it were, this image within himself, taking over their behaviour and standards. The child with warm, loving, wise, and accepting parents incorporates them as individuals not imposing impossible standards but providing ideals within the bounds of the attainable.

So, from being creatures only concerned with their own demanding drives and impulses, children begin to develop as per-sons in relation to others and their feelings and needs.

William James suggests that a person's self is the 'sum total of all that he can call his own'.

If we are the result of all our yesterdays, are unique individuals trailing our personal 'clouds of glory', we also trail our ancestors behind us, the savages, labourers, skilled workmen, artists, thieves, murderers and destroyers.

Certainly environment is of immense importance and many

children are handicapped from the very beginning by the poverty, meagreness, unsuitability and instability of their background. Yet at the same time we cannot ignore our past.

One might ask at what age do we begin to see ourselves as persons, individuals different from everyone else?

Obviously it must happen to different people at different times in their lives when they discover their own uniqueness, their identity and their own definition of who and what they are.

R. D. Laing speaks of a man having 'a sense of his presence in the world as a real, alive whole, and in a temporal sense a continuous person. As such he can live out into the world and meet others : a world and others experienced as equally real, alive, whole and continuous.'[1]

Sometimes an individual is thrust into selfhood, unexpectedly and suddenly. Anne Frank in her book *The Diary of a Young Girl* in the forcing yet isolated world of the annexe in which she and her Jewish family hid during the German occupation of Holland writes, 'After I came here when I was just 14 I began to think about myself sooner than most girls and to know that I am a person. Sometimes when I lie in bed at night I have a terrible desire to feel my breasts and to listen to the quiet rhythmic beat of my heart.'[2]

Emily, in Richard Hughes's book *A High Wind in Jamaica* suddenly becomes aware of her own selfhood in an unexpected place :

She had been playing houses in a nook in the bows behind the windlass, it suddenly flashed into her mind that she was she. . . .

She stopped dead and began looking over all of her person which came within range of eyes. She could not see much, except a fore-shortened view of the front of her frock and her hands when she lifted them for inspection.

She began to laugh, rather mockingly. 'Well,' she thought, in effect 'Fancy *you*, of all people going and getting caught like this!—You can't get out of it now, not for a very long time; you'll have to go through with this being a child, and growing up, and getting old, before you'll be quit of this mad prank!'. . . .

Determined to avoid any interruptions of this highly important occasion, she began to climb the ratlines, on her way to her favourite perch on the mast-head. . . .

Once settled on her perch, she began examining the skin of her hands with the utmost care : for it was Hers. She slipped a shoulder out of the top of her frock; and having peeped in to make sure she was really continuous under her clothes, she shrugged it up to touch her cheek. The contact of her face and the warm bare hollow of her shoulder gave her a comfortable thrill, as if it was the caress of some kind friend. But whether the feeling came to her through her cheek or her shoulder, which was the caresser and which the caressed, that no analysis could tell her.

Once fully convinced of this astonishing fact, that she was Emily Bas-Thornton . . . she began seriously to reckon its implications.

First, what agency had so ordered it that out of all people in the world who she might have been, she was this particular one, this Emily : born in such-and-such a year out of all the years in Time, and encased in this particularly pleasing little casket of flesh.

Secondly . . . She had been alive for over ten years now and it had never once entered her head'.[3]

So both Anne and Emily had become aware of themselves in relation to their bodies as the core of their being in a rather special way, an awareness that had developed gradually and now thrust itself upon them in time and space, an awareness that children are learning all the time in their day-to-day activity.

The mentally sick child or adult often does not see himself in his body at all but as an isolated object viewed from the outside, unable therefore to participate or share in the things that happen in the real world. Whatever strange relationship does exist between such an individual and his body it becomes extremely involved and complex.

The autistic child, about whom we really know so little, appears to be locked away in a terrifying, secret world which only he inhabits with no bridge to reality.

Like the other life tasks presented to children, selfhood is bound up with the need to develop as an individual person and not just an appendage of the family or the establishment in which they happen to be born or live. So the growth of independence in children is a very necessary and important objective. Obviously with very young children there are decisions which can only be made by the adult; health and safety may be involved, or certain necessary patterns of social behaviour about which they lack knowledge and experience. However, things are often forbidden for no valid reason; 'because I say so', says the grownup casting his authoritarian mantle over the child.

It must always be remembered too, that different societies expect and demand different roles from their members; what is wicked and immoral in one culture is normal and acceptable in another and this will obviously produce different personalities. If, however, children are prevented from developing into independent personalities they will become like an over-rigid culture which relies solely on ancient taboos and customs and which disintegrates when suddenly faced with exciting novelties. This has happened to many primitive races; they have vanished almost completely leaving little behind to show that they once existed as a people in their own right. Children unaccustomed to freedom, to independence, to making decisions for themselves, can be bewildered, frightened and stampeded into foolish behaviour when suddenly faced with situations which are new and unexpected.

Children in their day-to-day living need practice in learning to be independent and to make decisions. This can be done largely, in the early stages, through their play. They choose what they will play with and how long they will continue, how to arrange, organize and plan what they are doing, whom they will play with, where they will play, and so on.

This may appear very simple as far as we are concerned for to us these are often unimportant matters; to a child they can be momentous because to him play is the whole object of his life. He may at times ask and welcome our help or even share his play with us and we on our part can often enrich his activities by what we provide materially, or the ideas we can bring or the questions we can answer. We should not, however, take over and organize *what* he is doing, for that is for him to do.

It is not surprising perhaps that life is often a difficult and complicated affair for most children, with problems enough without our inventing more through lack of understanding and wisdom. Most of us, too, are well aware of the growth tasks that still face us and the difficulties we also experience in coming to terms with them.

3
Primitive play materials

Play, based as it is on the acceptance of symbols, has infinite possibility in it. It enables the child to experience whatever is to be found in his or her personal inner psychic reality, which is the basis of the growing sense of identity. There will be aggression there as well as love.

D. W. WINNICOTT, *The Child, the Family, and the Outside World*

All play is bound up with emotion, feelings of pleasure and fulfilment, unhappiness and anxiety, guilt and frustration. Most play materials that children use serve all sorts of purposes and cater for all sorts of different needs. Many of the simpler and more primitive ones do appear to provide particularly satisfactory outlets for children's feelings of love and hate, hostility and destruction, messing and dirtying; and all children the world over have these feelings.

Aggression is a very necessary and valuable impulse for it provides the driving force which enables us to deal with the problems and difficulties that life is continually facing us with. It is the aim and purpose for which we use this drive that matters.

Children feel aggressive and hostile towards both people and objects: objects because they get in the way or will not behave as the child wishes; parents and other adults because they are frustrating and demanding. They expect him to do things he does not want to, they deny him pleasures he feels he has a right to enjoy.

The hostility he feels towards his parents, however, is combined with his feelings of love and dependence. He needs them very badly. He cannot do without their affection and care. Who would provide him with all the things he needs, comfort him and treasure him, give him treats and presents and protect him from danger? Parents are the most important things in a child's world; without them he is utterly lost. This makes his anger and hate very difficult to accept and understand.

He is often jealous and resentful of his brothers and sisters. Sometimes when they are able to do things he cannot manage and he tries in vain to compete with them, he may show his feelings in all sorts of hostile ways.

Obviously aggression will take different forms at different ages. The young child may indulge in temper tantrums when he is thwarted or he may displace the anger that he feels towards his mother on to other children or on to his possessions. He may be quarrelsome and disagreeable with them and break and destroy his toys. This to him is a safer way of showing his anger than hurting and damaging the mother whom he loves and on whom he relies.

The understanding parent does not, of course, make a child feel he is being outrageously wicked when he is angry so that he is overcome by remorse and guilt. She will naturally prevent him from really hurting her or himself and protect his siblings or playmates from hostile attacks.

If a child is given the support and affection he needs when he is aggressive and angry he will be able to accept the fact that he possesses both creative and destructive impulses but he will not be made to feel his anger is so terrible that he must hide it away so that it never appears, or that it is far too dangerous even to contemplate. If a child is made to feel an outcast, and becomes terrified of his own hostility, he may withdraw completely into himself, unable to communicate or share in the lively, energetic play and the normal give and take which is part of children's spontaneous activity. Such children may, as they grow older, find it increasingly difficult to take their place in society, and underneath their extreme diffidence, self-depreciation and unresponsiveness may lurk powerful feelings of resentment and hate.

There is always a danger of driving emotion underground. As Jersild suggests,

A child learns to disguise his feelings, or to hide them or to express them in devious ways. Many children learn also to disapprove of themselves for having intense feelings. But they cannot rid themselves of these inborn and essential tendencies to be frightened, angry, grief-stricken and ashamed.

As a result from an early age many children are involved in a conflict within themselves, a struggle arising from the fact that they cannot help becoming angry, yet they should not show anger or feel it, they cannot help being frightened yet they should not be sissies or 'fraidy cats'. They are under pressure to play false with their feelings, and a child does this when he is seething with resentment against his elders but instead of showing this directly he breaks bottles on a public highway. . . . It is natural and healthy for a child to cry when hurt, to sob when in distress, to weep when lonely, to shriek with fright and to scream in anger if he is helpless in his rage.[1]

Play is one of the most important ways in which children learn that feelings can be safely expressed, that aggression and hostility can be controlled and managed and that its energy is available to be used constructively.

Primitive play materials, e.g. water, earth, sand, clay, mud, are particularly valuable for they not only link children with the actual substance of the world in which they live and have their involvement with forbidden bodily and sexual pleasures, but provide legitimate outlets for destructive play without making children feel guilty that they have broken or damaged something of value.

All these things can be maltreated in all sorts of ways : pounded, banged, pummelled, moulded, forced this way and that; yet nothing has been destroyed that cannot be put right again.

Often children feel that if they show hostility to a person or an object they must expect retaliatory behaviour—'an eye for an eye, a tooth for a tooth'—and they even feel an inanimate object may strike back. It is comforting therefore that primitive materials reassure children by their yielding pliability that they are in no way revengeful.

Children will often talk quite spontaneously while playing with such materials, showing perhaps an unexpected jealousy and anger towards siblings and parents, which obviously need a safe outlet. So when putting bits of clay or dough through a mincing machine, jumping on a sand-castle or slapping or moulding a mud pie, children are enabled in phantasy to identify these objects and acts with people and things that have angered and frustrated them.

Part of these feelings and one of the mechanisms at work in children's and adults' behaviour is that of projection. We all tend to project onto others our own badness and hostility, seeing all the wrong-doing in them while feeling ourselves and our friends to be the good and clever ones; as Susan Isaacs points out, 'Under cover of this projection of one's own evil onto others, little children will go far in real unkindness or even cruelty to the moral victim of the moment. They but exemplify, however, the profound moral aggression of society as a whole. Human history sets forth an unending tale of burning, maiming, killing, torturing, imprisonment and all the resources of human ingenuity in devising cruel revenge under the pressure of this mechanism.'[2]

William Golding in his novel *Lord of the Flies* gives a vivid picture of this mechanism at work in phantasy play. He shows how a group of apparently civilized boys wrecked on a desert island revert to primitive aggressive activity and behaviour. The group is divided and their hate and fear is projected onto two of the boys, Piggy and Ralph. Piggy is killed by being pushed off a high rock when he and Ralph are trying to persuade the other boys to less lawless and more constructive behaviour. Jack, the leader of the revolt, shouts triumphantly as Piggy dies. 'See? That's what you'll get! I meant that! There isn't a tribe for you any more! . . . I'm Chief.'

'Viciously, with full intention, he hurled the spear at Ralph. The point tore the skin and flesh over Ralph's ribs, then sheared off and fell into the water. Ralph stumbled, feeling not pain but panic, and the tribe, screaming now like the Chief, began to advance.'[3]

Therefore, to understand, master and use aggression wisely is something all children need to learn early.

At the pre-school stage, for example, if they can be helped to feel secure, the standards set them are reasonable and attainable and their play material suitable; their own growing confidence in themselves and their ability to make satisfactory relationships lessens their own internal conflicts and anxieties. So, their need to hate others because of their own faults becomes less urgent and the warm, tender and protective impulses, which all young children possess, gain ascendancy.

Some children, of course, may actually be lacking in determination and the ability to stick up for themselves and may need to be encouraged to use the most highly socialized form of defence of which they are capable at that particular moment.

A child may need to hold on to the toys with which he is playing but perhaps this is not enough. He may push the other child away, or he may resort to hitting and it would be a mistake at such a stage to prevent him from actively defending his own property. He may get hit back but he has to face the reality of the situation just as he must face the existing reality of his own aggression.

Sometimes a young or insecure child may need adult intervention to hold onto or retrieve a particular toy and support for his efforts. As a child grows older, gains in confidence, becomes more socialized and is able to use language more easily to express his wishes and talk to other children, the need to hit or strike others not only lessens, but would not receive encouragement and support from the adult.

Over-permissiveness, bullying, allowing a child to be needlessly destructive, can be very frightening to him and boys and girls despise the adult who cannot keep order.

When John in a temper broke a beloved toy he turned on his mother with tears running down his cheeks, saying pathetically and reproachfully, 'Why did you let me do it?'

The destructiveness of the very disturbed child will obviously differ from that of a normal child not only in quality but in the degree and kind of destructiveness employed.

Normal children destroy things, pull their toys to pieces, kick their bricks about, hit and pinch each other, scream and get angry. They do not, however, go on needlessly destroying; very soon their play becomes constructive and creative, they are sorry for their bad behaviour and want to make reparation, but they do not show exaggerated feelings of guilt.

The neurotic child, on the other hand, gets caught up in his own wanton destruction which he cannot control. Often his excitement mounts and although he may appear indifferent to what he is doing he obviously has strong feelings of anxiety and guilt about his behaviour.

There are naturally many different kinds of play material and types of activity which provide outlets for children's impulses as well as the more primitive materials mentioned.

Energetic and lively games of cops and robbers, and cowboys and Indians which young children indulge in, the challenging and more sophisticated activities of older boys and girls when they climb, race, build gang huts, dam streams, use planks and boxes in constructive play, all need drive and initiative.

Although not play in the true sense of the word, organized team games can be thought of as regulated aggressive behaviour, only tolerated when the rules are kept.

We have already seen the need for young children to come to terms with the feelings connected with early toilet-training. The mastering of this particular bodily skill is bound up with emotions of both love and hate.

Among the primitive play materials available water is one that appears to be closely linked with a child's interest in his own body products. Here is a legitimate substitute, for a child is able to equate water and urine. He is thus able to satisfy needs which present child-rearing fashions deny and frustrate.

Yet is water play so easily available for children today? So often we find that it is confined in polite fountains in city squares surrounded by concrete. It sprays tidy lawns and flowers beds, it is controlled in neat kitchen taps and sterile bathrooms to be used with care and circumspection.

Yet we are continually reminded that most children cannot leave water alone. They wade through large puddles whether they are wearing their wellingtons or their slippers. They turn on the taps in the most hygienic of kitchens and bathrooms and slop about in the water that fills sinks and basins and overflows onto the floor. They wash doll's clothes, scrub floors, blow bubbles, have water tea-parties; in fact, water in play form looms large in their lives which after all began in a bag of fluid.

Water is relaxing and undemanding for the tired and worried child. It can be repetitious and monotonous, dribbled through the fingers or cupped in the hands. Although it invites much intellectual thought and experiment there is no need for the child to accept this particular challenge if it is not desired. It is yielding and unresisting, cool and soothing, warm and comforting. Children need the sort of sensory experiences which water has the power to give.

Water, too, washes things clean, and this children find very comforting when they feel guilty about the mess they have made. Symbolically, as adults, we also try to wash away our guilt. 'What, will these hands ne'er be clean?' is Lady Macbeth's cry as she walks in her sleep, continually rubbing her hands as if washing them.

In considering, however, the deeper implications of water play one must not forget its pure pleasure and delight and here is Laurie Lee's discovery of water recollected from the excitement of childhood in his autobiography *Cider with Rosie.*

> Here [he says] I discovered water—a very different element from the green crawling scum that stank in the garden tub. You could pump it in pure blue gulps out of the ground. You could swing on the pump handle and it came out sparkling like liquid sky. And it broke and ran and shone on the tiled floor, or quivered in a jug, or weighted your clothes with cold. You could drink it, draw with it, froth it with soap, swim beetles across it, or fly it in bubbles in the air. You could put your head in it and open your eyes, and see the sides of the bucket buckle and hear your caught breath roar, and work your mouth like a fish, and smell the lime from the ground. Substance of magic—which you could tear or wear, confine or scatter or send down holes, but never burn or break or destroy.[4]

Some children may find messy play with primitive materials unpleasant and frightening. Their possibilities present dangers which are difficult to face or arouse emotions they feel they may not be able to manage.

They show repugnance at the sticky touch of wet clay, the oozy feel of mud and earth or the clinging quality of wet sand and they do not enjoy mixing water and sand together.

Perhaps the child who is trying to play safe and keep himself clean and tidy has never had either the encouragement or the opportunity to discover the satisfying pleasures in such materials. He may have been punished for getting himself dirty, perhaps his early toilet training has been strict and exacting, associated with strong feelings of guilt, naughtiness, fear and disapproval. Whatever we do we must not alienate children from their physical selves. Adult sexual behaviour and enjoyment is a messy affair and it is only too easy because of the way in which our bodies are made to associate sex and elimination and to make children feel that both are dirty and disgusting.

One must not exaggerate a withdrawal from messy play and see in it maladjustments that do not exist. Some children may be more fastidious than others, less aggressive, more generally placid so that the frustrations of life worry them less. There may be all sorts of other things they enjoy doing which provide outlets for their feelings. However, one would certainly take heed of the child who seemed abnormally troubled and anxious when faced with these materials.

4

Social relationships in play

When it is very young the infant's social play is directed primarily at the parents, but as it grows the emphasis is shifted from them towards other children of the same age. The child becomes a member of a juvenile 'play Group'. This is a critical step in development. As an exploratory involvement it has far reaching effects on the later life of the individual.

DESMOND MORRIS, *The Naked Ape*

The first relationship that a child experiences is the one that he has with his own mother (or mother substitute) and the importance of the quality of this first relationship cannot be over-estimated.

The growing baby who is loved, wanted, and accepted will tend to expect the world to be a friendly, kindly place and its inhabitants friendly, kindly people. The child who is rejected and unwanted will, on the other hand, often look with suspicion and hostility on a world that has shown so clearly that he is of little account in it. So, a child's first contact with other children will be coloured by his own early family relationships.

Children are eager for contacts with others round about their own age. Small babies in prams near together reach out to each other and even if they pull each other's hair, or snatch each other's rattles they do not necessarily mean to be hurtful; they are curious and excited about this moving object so close at hand.

Children's social play from the developmental angle has been classified under five main stages; solitary play, spectator play (when children are concerned in watching each other), parallel play when they like to be near each other, associative play when they often *appear* to be playing together, and genuine cooperative play.

Obviously, the age at which he reaches the various social stages in his play will depend to a certain extent on the play opportunities and social contacts a child has had.

Certainly the very young child will be mainly concerned with himself, his own toys, and the presence of a loved adult. He will very soon, however, begin to enjoy watching other children. If he is out in his pram or pushchair he will laugh, look around, and shout at what he sees going on where other boys and girls are concerned.

Watching others goes on at all ages and stages. Many children on first going to Nursery School or into a group of any kind are fearful of joining in the play they see going on around them and may watch for quite a long time. Although we may help them to join in they must not be hurried or forced to participate before they are ready.

Some children temperamentally are less outgoing than others and prefer to do things on their own. If they seem to be happy and well-adjusted, and can make normal contacts when needed, then one would not be anxious on their account. It is the child who seems withdrawn, afraid, and unhappy that might cause one some concern.

Children of round about two to three like playing near each other, often happily continuing with their own affairs, sometimes seemingly oblivious of those near them, yet sufficiently aware to notice if they are left all alone.

Not all children are willing to lend their toys to each other and two-year-olds particularly are not anxious to share; they will hold onto their possessions or firmly sit on them. This is very understandable. It is difficult to lend or give until one has really owned, especially for children who have never really possessed the thing they want most of all, their mother's love. There is also a very practical consideration; other children may break or destroy the toy they grab and the older child may know this and feel devastated at the thought of a favourite doll being broken. Possessions, too, are an extension of ourselves and our defined territories and so, important to us.

Some children feel that if they see a thing, think of a thing, or mention it first it is theirs. Others enjoy giving out, or ordering other children about with toys and materials even though they are communal property and not theirs.

Children's ultimate desire to own no doubt springs from their very first desire to have the exclusive possession of their mother and the food she provided and their fear and helplessness in this situation if their satisfactions were denied; so they feel it is vital to hold on to what they have and desire.

Rivalry in children's play again springs from this original fear of losing to others their rightful love and they see in other boys and girls a threat to their own unique position. Children often use the mechanism of displacement in their anger against other children. They are, perhaps, afraid to hit or abuse a child who has really incurred their jealous wrath, grabbed a toy, or torn their book and so they vent their anger on some weaker brethren.

Adults behave in much the same way. The boss reproves his manager for some mistake, and the manager takes it out on an innocent individual who is in some inferior position and who finds it difficult or impossible to retaliate.

A scapegoat is needed, we all unite against a common enemy or we find a minority group on which to vent our guilty anger. Children will pick on a child in their play, exclude him, taunt him, and generally make him feel an outcast, different from everyone and to blame for everything.

With groups of young children certain play materials make the beginnings of sharing easy and the overall secure and satisfying atmosphere that can exist in a group also helps children to be kind and friendly.

Play with sand, water, dressing-up clothes or large outdoor equipment can be just as satisfying for several children as for one. If there is only a single very popular toy—a tricycle, a pram, or a truck—children, who have no sense of time, imagine they will never get a turn. The only way of securing the longed-for object is to obtain it by force and they naturally expect the worst of other children as they know what they would do—hang on to the toy as long as possible. So, there are needless heartbreaks and disputes in their struggles to get it.

It can sometimes be helpful to children who seem to find

making easy play contacts very difficult, to suggest a few useful social techniques. If, for example, a child says 'If you don't let me play I'll hit you' he won't be welcome, but if he asks pleasantly or praises what he sees being done he will be far more likely to be kindly received.

If a child is always dropping the ball in a simple game or doing the wrong thing a little help in acquiring a particular skill may make all the difference in the world.

If, too, when the adult is taking two or three children along to see or do something rather special, the left-out child is included, this brings him quite naturally into the group.

When children have reached the stage of associative play, they are not only aware of each other but talk to each other and often appear to be playing together, as Susan Isaacs suggests : 'The play of a number of young children is little more than a congeries of individual phantasies. When these phantasies happen to overlap they give rise to common activity, and may for the time being weld the players together into a group. As the children get to know each other, and build up a common history, the mutual adoption of phantasy occurs more and more often. They gain the experience of doing things together in some way and some sense, and discover the benefits and delights of mutual support, both in imaginative play and in real achievement'.[1]

Thus, to begin with, group play among pre-school children is a very fluid affair. Small numbers come together, break up and change; temporary leaders appear and come and go. There are mature, dynamic children who do emerge as leaders. They are the ones who often initiate some play. Sometimes they organize the other children in a friendly way, thus preventing disagreement and quarrels. Some children are extremely sensitive to the needs and feelings of others and instinctively they seem to do the right thing.

The child with ideas will often be welcomed by the others simply because he discovers the solution to their problems, and suggests ways of coping with equipment so that the play is successful and satisfying to everyone.

Alan, at six a highly intelligent little boy, disliked quarrels and rough play and yet at the same time liked his own way. He was often very skilful at redirecting the other children's activities or making a suggestion that meant they forgot their arguments and went on to follow up the suggestions he had made, thus leaving him free to do what he wanted and to keep the things he had chosen to play with.

He had a very tactful way of admiring other children's efforts which often prevented arguments and he would then quickly go on with an idea to improve what they had done. The other children by then were often predisposed to accept his interference in their efforts.

Some children, of course, will just use others to satisfy their own individual phantasies, commanding them to do something or watch something they are doing. Sometimes the other children will comply, sometimes they will not, and then a child may have to fall back on an obliging adult.

As has already been suggested the working-class child has to learn early how to cope with others and avoid extensive quarrelling. Turned out into the street he must sink or swim : mother is not just behind him to support him and fight his battles; he must do this for himself. He must protect his own playthings or he will lose them. If he swops a good possession for a shoddy one he will have to bear the loss as best he can. On the whole, his mother needs to keep on good terms with her close-living neighbours and certainly wants to avoid unnecessary rows with them.

The middle-class child is protected socially to a much greater degree, plays in his own garden or playroom, invites his own friends in. Which way is of most value to the child is open to question; probably most children need a little of both.

Children playing freely with others in a group often get a share in being the leader even if they are not one all the time. Philip, a rather shy child, was able to organize and lead a group of the younger children and so get a taste of what leadership involved. When he played with the big boys and girls he was just a follower, running after them and doing what they suggested. He enjoyed this immensely and had the opportunity of active play with big boys and girls from which he was able to learn quite a lot.

The value children get from playing with each other is immense, for here is the real clash of wills among equals. The adult tends either to take over and organize a child's play completely, giving him no chance to try out things, make mistakes and work out his own phantasies, or to obey his every whim meekly and obediently so that there is no challenge to himself as an individual.

Hostility and aggression in children's play together includes the desire for possession and power and feelings of rivalry, inferiority and superiority. These feelings are perhaps easier to accept if we remember that they spring from a child's earliest feelings in relation to his family, even though consciously the child is quite unaware of this.

Boys and girls naturally show their animosity in unpleasant ways by biting, hitting, spoiling each others' work, snatching toys and using verbal threats, and this sort of behaviour, though differing in the way in which it is conducted, can also be seen among adults.

Teasing can be disagreeable and although one can say that 'hard words break no bones' behind these verbal threats children often sense something more formidable. 'Your painting is horrid', can mean 'it's better than mine and I'm going to tear yours up'. 'That's a silly castle', implies that the other child is going to jump on it and destroy it.

Children's need for power in their social play is a reflection of their own inadequate feelings about themselves as they do things to others that have been done to them by the adult world.

On the whole, however, young children's quarrels are short-lived. Their aggression towards each other is a part of development; it shows at least recognition of another child and is a more constructive attitude than a mere passive reaction; there is more feeling in an attack than in just hostile watching. If adults show a protective attitude to children, their influence will be felt and we all know how the good teacher can create a feeling of sympathy, warmth and understanding by her own example in a group of children.

Although boys and girls can often be left to settle their own minor quarrels in their play, the adult must see that there is no bullying and that teasing does not reach the stage when a child is really upset or terrorized.

Even with young children one can get sexual rivalries, if for example there are two boys and one girl or two girls and one boy, and verbal taunts and jealous bickering can be difficult and disruptive in a group.

As children get older, at the five- to seven-year-old stage they begin to play cooperatively together, more aware of each other's needs and wishes and the contribution another child can make to their play. Other children are, in fact, fun to play with, useful and helpful, less of a menace, because by this time children feel more secure within themselves.

Real cooperation does of course have its ups and down and six-year-olds in particular sometimes seem to go through a contrary and quarrelsome stage; and though happily playing together at some times, at others can resort to spiteful and unkind behaviour, a regression to earlier forms of social play.

In spite of all these anti-social feelings which young children express, they often get on very well together particularly in a rich and challenging environment, with knowledgeable adults at hand to care and help them. They are often very understanding of each other's needs and really want each other's company. They will comfort each other, offer help and say they are sorry quite spontaneously if they have hurt another child. They will often admire each other's efforts in a very generous way. The four- and five-year-olds will take charge of a younger child sometimes, of course, overwhelming him with kindness and affectionate care but at the same time providing support and comfort in a new situation.

They are prepared to accept, almost without question, children whose colour, clothes and culture are different from their own and it is only as they grow older that they unfortunately often take over the intolerant attitudes and behaviour that they find around them in the adult world.

Desmond Morris reminds us that 'It has been found that aggressiveness can be increased by raising the density of a group of children. Under crowded conditions the friendly, social interactions between members of a group become reduced and the destructive and aggressive patterns show a marked rise in frequency and intensity.'[2]

As human beings we find it difficult to live together in huge numbers for we began in small tribal groups and this is what we can really manage. Yet life is continually forcing us to make contact with large numbers of our kind in our travels, our work and our leisure. We have, therefore, built up a series of behaviour patterns which helps us to avoid personal contacts. This makes it possible to exist in situations which would otherwise be appallingly over-stimulating. This, no doubt, is something which should be carefully considered in bringing together large groups of young children. It is also a pointer to much of the aggression of today; when children live in overcrowded conditions and when parents and children have no privacy, no place for their own pursuits, no room for their own belongings, and from a very early age there are no real play facilities, their aggressive and hostile impulses are not only over-stimulated but continually being reinforced and recharged.

Children need to be able to play in small groups so that they get to know each other and are not overwhelmed by the actual number of running, moving, challenging, touching bodies which seethe and shout around them in a never-ending way.

One of the intellectual attainments intimately connected with social development, which separates man from the animal world, is our ability to communicate in language, perhaps one of our greatest achievements.

Round about two the average child has a vocabulary of about 300 words or even more and by five well over the 2,000 mark will have been reached.

The normal baby has an innate ability to make all the sounds that are known to mankind. He uses and continually experiments with these sounds in his babbling and gradually those that he will need in his own particular culture will sort themselves out from the rest and will become the predominant ones because they are the sounds he hears around him all the time. The acquiring of language not only helps children to gain control over their impulses, it helps them to understand and manage their environment if they are able to name the things they see around them.

Through language a child can make his wishes known and perhaps fulfilled. Through it he can begin to express his feelings even if at first he does so very inadequately. He can to some extent satisfy his curiosity by asking questions and understanding the answers when things are explained to him. He experiences frustration and stress less when he hears the reasons behind a particular demand.

To be unable either to understand or be understood is a devastating experience and we as adults often feel lost and uneasy when in a strange country we do not comprehend a word we hear spoken. Ronith, a four-year-old who spoke Hebrew and came with his parents to England, went to Nursery School and said rather pathetically to his mother after his first few days there: 'Mother, they don't understand me when I open my mouth.' He could not grasp that when he spoke in his own language to the other children they did not know what he was saying.

Children do not talk in a vacuum and even the adult deprived of the company of his fellows, stranded on a desert island or in solitary confinement, forgets how to express himself and on returning to civilization discovers that his normal speech is hesitant, awkward, lacking in fluency and purpose. Children delight in the encouragement and praise that the adult gives them as they learn to talk, but because speech is closely linked with feeling they must be secure and at home with the adults and the other children they are with.

Children need not only other children to talk and play with, but also an environment and play material which encourage conversation and experiment of all kinds, for an empty playroom would provide little incentive for lively and spontaneous talk and play.

As adults we need to bring to children's play interesting things for them to use, look at, discuss, handle—feathers for an Indian head-dress, flowers and shells for a garden, a telephone for the house corner.

Practitioner role

We listen to children's questions, requests, explanations, descriptions of their paintings, their buildings, their dressing-up play. We share their enthusiasms and excitements, their laughter and achievements. We suggest, welcome and comment in words and sentences. We tell and read stories and poetry, we sing songs and share picture books. All this adds to the richness of children's play and their language development as a whole.

Children talk to each other, they talk to themselves regardless of who is there, but an audience can be useful even if the other child is not really listening, though we have already seen how important at all stages of social play other children are.

To put something into words, to verbalize phantasy, helps children to understand and control it. They discover too that social relationships become easier and more friendly when, for example, they can ask for a toy rather than snatch it, suggest that a child gives them some room on the table to play, rather than push his things roughly aside, or ride roughshod over his activities and wishes.

Because language is based on concrete experience and personal relationships, the day-to-day play of children is the basis for their language development. Without words to string their days and lives together they will be at the mercy of every strange wind that blows.

5

Imaginative and dramatic play

. . . the inner world of the mind has a continuous living reality of its own, with its own dynamic laws and characteristics, different from those of the external world.

SUSAN ISAACS, *The Nature and Function of Phantasy*

Dramatic play, and in a certain sense all play is dramatic, acts as it were as a mirror, for, as a child plays he is showing us (if we can understand) many of the facets of himself displayed in a variety of different ways and forms as he 'externalizes his inner drama, the various aspects of his inner personality'.

He is sorting out the world of reality and phantasy and discovering the point at which they spill over into each other and separate. He plays out past experiences and present problems and in putting them outside himself in his play he is able to see them more clearly and so lessen some of the anxieties and tensions within himself.

Perhaps it is because 'Man is a make-believe animal—he is never so truly himself as when he is acting a part'[1] that children act out in their play what both the inner world of themselves and the outer world of people and things mean to them. Language, valuable and helpful as it can be, is of little use to the young child for he has neither the ability nor the vocabulary to put his feelings into words.

The functions of dramatic play are many and varied. Children are able to imitate what they see going on around them and this reassures them as to the purpose and the meaning of the adult

adult life

world. They can discover what it is like and in so doing feel that they can understand and manage it more easily. They take over adult rôles, playing out themes and situations that have special significance for them and they practise in their play some of the tasks they will perform in real life when they are older.

The small girl gains some idea of what it will feel like to be a mother as she plays with her dolls, caring for them, dressing them and putting them to bed. In primitive societies small girls very soon find themselves helping with younger brothers and sisters in the real situation and their own time for play is sometimes very brief.

Small boys, too, need to act out masculine rôles and play at the things they see men doing in the world around them. Some small boys unfortunately miss a great deal when they have no chance of seeing their fathers at work. 'He' goes off to the office or factory in the morning and returns late at night and so his children have no share in his working life and his small son cannot proudly imitate his father or boast about his achievements.

'Who is that man who has breakfast with us on Sunday?' murmured a three-year-old whose father, involved in the executive and business world, hardly ever saw him and would never have dreamed of talking about what he did to justify his existence and bring home the money.

At the under-five stage there is a good deal of overlap in the kind of play boys and girls indulge in; some boys for instance like playing with dolls, some girls prefer engines and guns, often each like both.

Nowadays fathers do much more in the home than they used to : they wash up, cook, take the baby out; mothers may have jobs and go out to work, so children see less differences between the daily lives of their parents.

A certain amount of social pressure is exerted as children get older. Boys are encouraged to be masculine and girls feminine in their play and behaviour.

It is not at the moment always easy at first glance to distinguish between the sexes. Boys wear their hair long and dress up in fancy clothes while girls' slacks and jackets often look very masculine. Does this, one wonders, confuse children?

In any case one should never prevent or make children feel

they are being silly or babyish if they play with the toys we consider inappropriate to their sex.

Both boys and girls play out the things they see happening in their own homes, imitating the people they know best, taking over a gesture or a phrase, a way of walking or behaving which is a parental characteristic.

Mothers who fuss over their children's manners, food or health may see their own attitudes and feelings appearing in their child's play, showing the relationship between the child's life at home and the way he acts out what is happening there.)

One must not jump to the conclusion that the child who smacks and shakes her doll unmercifully is necessarily beaten by her mother at home. Children are often merely working through their own feelings of guilt in relation to their own bad behaviour and projecting it onto their dolls. They also get a pleasant feeling of power when they are able to act as a punishing adult. A destructive and aggressive child often finds comfort in playing at being kind and loving while a quiet and withdrawn child alternatively finds solace and an outlet for some of the pent-up hostility he is afraid to show openly to others in pretending to be a fierce biting lion or a cruel robber.

Older children often find playing with puppets or masks and spontaneous acting a safe outlet for their feelings; puppets can be made to say and do things that would be unacceptable in day-to-day behaviour. Behind a mask a child can hide his identity and in dressing up and acting out scenes he can take over the personality of some quite objectionable character and behave in a completely anti-social way without feeling guilty.

A child can even act out and talk about a physical handicap which he is both sensitive about and even ashamed of. Dressing up and playing a part often help him to accept this handicap more easily. It may be remembered that when the Brontë children were very young and their father wanted to discover how much they knew by questioning, he provided each child with a mask so that they felt less inhibited and freer to say what they really thought.

Children's jokes often show their mixed feelings about a person or situation. Something said seemingly in fun, with humour and laughter, could not be expressed in ordinary conversation. A child's conscious attitude may appear to be friendly and loving, but unconsciously he may feel very differently, so he expresses his hostility in a laughing, playful way which appears harmless and inoffensive.

This probably happens when children are playing at schools and pretending to be the teacher. Laughingly they make her do and say all sorts of impossible things. No doubt they would be afraid to say them to her face; in a pretend game of school, however, everything becomes possible.

Dressing-up clothes can often stimulate dramatic play and add to the fun of being a fireman, a nurse or a bride. Play becomes more realistic and richer in content as children remember how these characters behave, adding, of course, ideas of their own. If there are only dressing up garments which are going to appeal mainly to girls, boys will not have that extra incentive and stimulation that masculine attire can provide. If suitable things are there they will seize them with delight and use them to enrich their play.

Small children often enjoy just walking about dressed up without necessarily acting out the characters they are supposed to represent; in any case their dressing-up clothes are often a strange mixture of whatever comes to hand.

Dressing up does enable children to exhibit themselves to others in a rather special way; they are someone more than themselves, a little larger than life, and they can be noticed and admired. Certain clothes stand for certain characters, for everyone knows that if you wear a crown you are a king or a queen. There is a feeling, too, of power over others if, by dressing up as a ghost, for example, other children will be scared; and in some cases the scared children enjoy it as much as the scarer.

The boys in William Golding's novel, *Lord of the Flies*, already referred to, alone on their desert island, discarded their clothes, pretended to be savages and smeared themselves with clay to represent warpaint. It was at this stage, however, that they became so completely involved in their play that they also discarded their normal behaviour and began to behave like real savages; caught up in their phantasy play it all became larger than life. Unfortunately at this stage there was no helpful and understanding adult available to remind them that after all this was only play, only the world of make-believe; they were not really savages and so could not behave as if they were and the time had come to wash away the war paint.

Children are often able to accept all sorts of imaginative substitutes in their play which can offset some of the frustrations they have to experience. They will turn on imaginary taps, drink imaginary cups of tea, use bricks, beads or any handy object as food and so have exciting tea-parties with nothing real to eat or drink.

The outer trappings of the real world are unnecessary; a few boxes can make a home corner, a row of chairs becomes a bus or a train, a pile of bricks and planks an airport or a railway station.

Children are extremely understanding of the adult's unadaptable mind. 'It's only pretend cake' said a four-year-old as he offered a small brick on a plate to a grown-up, fearing perhaps she would be disappointed when she realized she couldn't eat it.

The dramatization and acting out of fears and anxieties enable children to understand them and come to terms with them more easily. On the whole adults are able to talk about their problems, but young children find this very difficult for they have neither the vocabulary nor the command of language which makes this possible or satisfying.

The frightened or unhappy child can sob or cry and show us his desolation and perhaps get comfort from the fact that a loving adult is there to console and help him.

Once an immediate danger or fear has for the moment vanished, a child needs to be able to bring this particular anxiety out into the open in his play in a situation in which he is in control. During the war (1939–45) many children who spent the night in shelters listening to the crash of falling bombs also spent a lot of their play in acting out these scenes. They would build imaginary air-raid shelters with tables and blankets, then hurry everyone into them, shouting that the bombs were falling. They would play endless shooting and bombing games accompanying them with as many appropriate sounds as possible.

While their parents put into words their latest and most harrowing bomb story the children put it into their play.

Martin, who had had a narrow escape one night when a bomb

fell unpleasantly close and broken glass showered in on the family as they were having a snack in the kitchen, played the whole scene out in Nursery School next day in a very noisy and vigorous way and then did a most colourful painting about it all.

War games of this kind disappeared almost overnight when the real war came to an end and it was no longer a present, living anxiety and fear in the children's mind.

Playing at doctors, pretending to give injections and administer medicine, is a safe way of re-enacting a really unpleasant episode. It is difficult to imagine the extent of the trauma that can be involved and the fear and pain some young children experience with the strange assaults on their own bodies which take place when they are ill and which they do not understand. One can only watch their play afterwards and wonder a little what it signifies, hoping its healing qualities will prevail.

Some parents find it rewarding to help their children play out situations that they know they are going very shortly to face. A visit to the hospital, the doctor or the dentist can be acted out beforehand so that some idea of what is going to happen is experienced. This does not necessarily mean that a child is able to accept the frightening situation stoically when it does arise; all of us are often quite brave before the event and the child may still be very frightened.

Because, however, the known is often far less terrifying than the unknown and what we imagine is so much worse than the reality, it does help children to have things played out or explained to them as clearly as possible. The child who is suddenly snatched from home without a word of explanation because mother is ill or the child who finds himself in a children's home and has no idea what the future holds, becomes a prey to a nightmare of imagined fears which may even be groundless and far worse than the reality of the situation.

Round about the age of three some children invent an imaginary companion to whom they will give a very special name. This imaginary companion can represent all sorts of things, often the bad bits of the child himself. It is not he who pinches the new baby or eats the sweets, but his imaginary companion. Such companions are often so real they must be given a place at table and taken for walks. Some children need thus to people their world, to compensate for real deprivations, endowing bits of themselves with very special qualities to comfort and support them.

Just as to possess an imaginary companion helps a child to feel that he is not alone in his goodness or badness, so in play to pretend to be one of the clever, powerful grownups who do so many wonderful things (drive trains, build houses, do the shopping, cook the dinner) helps to compensate for his feelings of smallness and inferiority. The world is full of large people and immense animals with everything geared, in fact, to an environment of giants.

It is difficult to realize how enormous the world of people and things must appear to a small child. Laurie Lee describes very vividly how he remembered feeling lost in a summer field one hot day. 'The June grass among which I stood, was taller than I was, and I wept. I had never been so close to grass before. It towered above me and all round me, each blade tattooed with tigerskins of sunlight. It was knife-edged, dark and a wicked green, thick as a forest and alive with grasshoppers that chirped and chattered and leapt through the air like monkeys. I was lost and I didn't know where to move. . . . I was lost and I did not expect to be found again.'[2]

Many of us have had the experience of returning to a house or garden we knew as children. Our memories tells us how huge it all was : towering trees and a forest of bushes, endless stretches of grass, large rooms, echoing stairs, dark passages, a palace of a home. Then we see it again through adult eyes. The trees and bushes are stunted, the grass a mere pocket handkerchief, the rooms poky, the passages short and narrow. An experience such as this gives some idea of a child-sized world.

The world of magic is a strange and wonderful one to a child. When wishes and words have such power that one has only to want or speak and––lo and behold !––it has all come to pass just as was desired.

Once when two-year-old Alison was extremely angry with everyone for going out on a picnic which she could not share she threatened firmly : 'I'm going to make it night and then you can't go' and she closed her eyes tightly convinced that it was now no longer day, everything was plunged in darkness, and the family would have to stay at home.

Edmund Gosse describes how his mind took refuge in an infantile species of natural magic. 'I formed', he said, 'strange super-stitions, which I can only render intelligible by naming some concrete examples. I persuaded myself that, if I could only dis-cover the proper words to say or the proper passes to make, I could induce the gorgeous birds and butterflies in my Father's illustrated manuals to come to life, and fly out of the book, leaving holes behind them. . . . I was convinced too that if I could only count consecutive numbers long enough, without losing one, I should suddenly, on reaching some far distant figure, find myself in possession of the great secret.'[3]

There can be anxiety and terror linked with this feeling of power in one's wishes. Suppose in a temper a child shouted 'I wish you were dead' to his mother and father and then this really happened.

Often when a loved parent dies children are overcome with feelings of guilt. Is it because they have been so naughty and at times wished their parents out of the way and hated them that this dreadful thing has happened?

This can be made even more difficult if adults hide their own grief, never talking about the dead person, or if they do, talking only in terms of their marvellous goodness and perfection. Not only is this an unnatural way of thinking about anyone but it makes the child feel even worse for he will remember how he felt and that at times he thought them hateful and unfair. Now he can never make amends and say he is sorry for his badness.

In the early stages of adult grief we all wish we had been more loving and understanding of the lost person and reproach our-selves for, perhaps, neglecting to ensure proper medical attention and care, or for the impatience and anger we sometimes felt and showed. Funeral rites and the often elaborate details involved are to the adult a way of seeing his grief, of acting it out openly, and looking at it in time and space.

A funeral for a dead pet with all the play that is involved in digging a grave, making a headstone, planting flowers, even singing seemingly quite inappropriate songs or nursery rhymes, helps children in the same way and their very real grief finds some kind of creative release.

Make-believe play, therefore, when children bring into the day-light of awareness some of their dark death fears at a level they can grasp makes them realize that they can pretend things that do not really exist and that their wishes are not all-powerful. So they play at death and disaster, funerals and weddings with equal fervour and enthusiasm.

Children are always using objects in the world around them as symbols to express their feelings and thoughts which otherwise would be unacceptable both to themselves and to the group in which they are living; we have already discussed how water and clay often symbolize for children urine and faeces. Although children may use phantasy play as an escape from reality because, overwhelmed by life, fear, anxiety, guilt and unhappiness, they withdraw into an elaborate world of their own because it is more satisfying than the real world in which they feel they are managing so badly, the most important function of phantasy play is that it enables children to resolve some of their conflicts at an unconscious level.

The under-five is unaware consciously that he is coming to terms with his feelings about wetting and soiling as he pours and dribbles water or squeezes his moist clay; that he is working through his feelings of anger and hostility to his parents, or substitute parents, when he paints a picture of crashing cars or cops and robbers fighting together.

Sometimes we may feel that the symbols a child unconsciously uses are absurd and far-fetched, but this is not so to the child. The world of symbolism is a strange and unfamiliar one and if we remembered and could interpret our own dreams we should be amazed at the bizarre objects we have selected from the real world to stand in as symbols for the unacceptable and unacknowledged bits of ourselves.

An important aspect of phantasy play and the way in which it differs from imaginative and dramatic play is that children are very aware when they are playing that reality and make-believe are two very different things, and they can slip without effort very easily from one to the other. In true phantasy play they are deeply committed, caught up in a world which blots out everything else and like the boys in William Golding's *The Lord of the Flies,* they are out of this world altogether. All children and adults too, have a foot in both worlds, the world of magic and phantasy and the world of reality, for in spite of what we

may think animistic beliefs survive in all of us. Shakespeare, for example, had no need to stress the supernatural because he was well aware that his audience accepted it and believed in it.

It is not difficult, therefore, for even the older child to become carried away into a world of phantasy, not only in individual play but in group play where he is able to find the solidarity of the group behind him; this is particularly true of the child over five who gravitates much more easily to play with other children.

So boys and girls use this group phantasy play which has perhaps been triggered off by something in the environment yet which seems to fit and symbolize an inner situation and need which cannot be accepted at the reality level. It may be the kind of phantasy play in which the group can deal with their angry feelings by finding a scapegoat in the outside world. As they are able to understand these feelings better and are no longer at their mercy, the need for a victim lessens. They can carry their own sins. Their play then often becomes much more peaceful and constructive.

Although, on the whole, group phantasy play is more usual with children over five, one does find it occurring with younger children as well.

Andrew was a disturbed child. When he was nearly two years old his mother had a new baby and the father deserted them. When Andrew came to the Nursery School he would not even acknowledge the new baby's existence. He was afraid of anything broken, damaged or dirty. He was smearing lavatory walls, was very constipated and played very little except to make involved drawings with a biro. His drawings revealed a very active phantasy life peopled by some imaginary characters called Poppy, Purple, Tulip, Dandelion and, later on Bud, who represented his new baby brother. These figures had exciting adventures with much aggressive action, and other children in the Nursery School group became interested, then began to take the names and act the parts out in character. Andrew was drawn into the play, at first almost without being aware of it, then he began to derive satisfaction from the contacts with others although he always withdrew if the children became noisy or quarrelsome.

He became much less frightened, accepted his brother who

was 'Bud', and began to use paint, water and sand although he never got very dirty. He was a very intelligent child and the other children were giving him a great deal of help by their reliance on his intellectual and imaginative stimulation in their play activities. What is more important is that, through play, Andrew was able to escape from his purely phantasy world and to face reality because in adopting these phantasy figures the other children had made them real for him[4].

In watching children's activities we are aware of several levels of behaviour. There is the conscious attitude to the adult, the other children and their physical environment, and there is the use of these people and objects to express unconscious attitudes to other things, other people and other situations. The 'Here and Now' has in it the past, the present and the future. . . .

We have seen too that children symbolize their thoughts and feelings by seeing an analogy in the outside world. In using the objects of the external world to symbolize their inner attitudes and ideas they are brought into contact with reality and learn much more about the objective world. A child whose contact with outside things is limited, is thrown back upon himself and the subjective element of thinking and feeling may be over-developed so that his thoughts and feelings lack the robustness and vitality that wide experience of the objective world and the people and things in it give.[5]

It is obvious, therefore, how much children, through their phantasy and imaginative play, learn about the real world as well as about their own inner one. As can be seen by Andrew's play, a child who is deeply involved with his own inner difficulties can be so overwhelmed by them he finds contacts with reality difficult and sometimes impossible.

Stable and happy children, on the other hand, find the outside world intriguing. They play at the things they have seen happening and a trip to an airport, a railway station or a market provides them with all sorts of exciting material.

Rich experiences therefore are vitally important and necessary and the child, confined, for example, in a large block of flats or in one small overcrowded room, who is rarely taken out and knows none of the delights of shared outings or neighbourhood visits, has missed a great deal which not only enriches the present but provides for the future.

Children watch, they ask questions, they listen, touch, feel and smell. They add their own drama to what they discover, taking from an experience what they are ready for and able to absorb. When their knowledge fails they add their own bits of make-believe so that the play is satisfying to them. They go to books and magazines for information and look at pictures and objects. They plan, discuss, make, build and talk. A game of Cowboys and Indians may well lead to a desire to find out more about their real lives, to the making of Indian head-dresses, cowboy belts and so on. Small boys often rush delightedly about pretending to be aeroplanes after a visit to an airport, but it also inspires a good deal of creative and constructive play.

Every creative achievement is born in the imagination and its form will depend on the individual who brings it to fruition. Shelley speaks of the imagination as being 'The greatest instrument for moral good'. So, if children are to understand the feelings and needs of others, they must be able to share imaginatively in their lives. In so doing they will not be content to stand back and do nothing if active help and comfort is needed.

The power to recall in memory things we have seen, heard, or done is extremely important and we could not develop without it. It may be a very simple memory that a child recalls, the place of a toy, the plot of a story, or a much more painful one, a visit to the hospital or dentist.

Dorothy Burlingham and Anna Freud describe how one of the children in their residential nursery would only let herself be held and fondled by someone she could not see. Sitting on an adult's lap she would enjoy the sensation of being held closely, but she always turned away her head so that in her own mind she could have an imaginary picture of her own mother. When she looked at the face of the person who was holding her she always burst into tears.[6] So this small child's love and need for her mother was being kept actively alive in her mind through the imaginative image she was able to evoke.

Children bring a freshness and a spontaneity to their imaginative play and a sense of wonder and delight which has its own special quality, a quality which is unfortunately so easy to lose as they grow older; yet this ability is needed in later life. We use our imaginations to solve problems, thinking ahead so as to envisage what may happen, to foresee possibilities and to imagine the kind of experiences that are needed; all this is of vital importance as much to the scientist as to the creative artist or writer. To cut out of children's education, therefore, those subjects which feed and stimulate the imaginative life is to impoverish their whole education.

6

Painting and brick building

The thing which I understand by real art is the expression by man of pleasure in labour.

WILLIAM MORRIS

Although one cannot divide children's play into neat, watertight compartments their play paintings do seem to have something both delightfully creative and very revealing about them, that as Herbert Read suggests, 'fully integrates both perception and feeling'. Perhaps it is helpful too that there are no right or wrong ways of painting as far as young children are concerned and therefore they do not feel inhibited or restricted in any way.

We can look at children's paintings in different ways. There is the developmental angle where we can see the various stages a child is passing through, and there is the one that tells us about him as an individual, how he feels about himself and the world of people and things.

Rhoda Kellogg in her study of thousands of children's drawings from all over the world saw five main developmental stages with 20 types of scribble which she called the 'building blocks of art'. Naturally one stage merged and ran into the next as children went forward and then regressed in their drawings. Round about two years of age children acquire the ability to make placement patterns which means that the marks on their paper fall into recognizable patterns often combined with basic scribble.[1]

From the patterned stage a child enters the shape stage in which emerging and definite diagrams such as *mandalas*, suns and radials occur; then comes pictorial work, humans, animals, buildings and so on.

The *mandala* shows itself in children's early drawings and also in adult art, and it is interesting to see in many of the old masters this magic circle of wholeness and completeness appearing particularly in religious pictures of the Holy Family for in oriental religion the *mandala* represented the cosmos. (The word *mandala* comes from a Sanscrit word meaning 'circle'.)

In speaking of *mandalas* Rhoda Kellogg defines them as 'a key part of the sequences that leads from abstract work to pictorials'. From *mandalas* a child goes on to draw suns and humans always incorporating into his new drawings aspects of his previous work; however crude this may appear to us there is a logical and visual system of development The mandaloid shape which forms the basis for a child's drawing of the human form also acts as a link between child and adult art. Jung feels that the *mandala* can be explained as inborn images, the collective unconscious, the timeless experience of the human race.

A child is able to integrate movement and vision. He distinguishes overall shapes, perceives details and old and new line formations. There is aesthetic pleasure as well as muscular satisfaction.

It is interesting to observe that the ancient symbols man has used to communicate with his fellows in writing are reflected in children's early drawings, and in patterns and diagrams which are similar all the world over.

As from a child's spontaneous scribble hand and eye coordination are promoted so, later on, when learning to read, he needs to interpret lines similar to those he has drawn; most of the letters he has to make have already appeared spontaneously in his pictures. Apart from the developmental sequences that children's paintings show there is the way in which they tell us about the children themselves. Obviously, at first, art is seen as a challenge, in that a child wants to investigate the possibilities of crayons, paints, pencils, etc. He discovers he can make his mark somewhere or cover some large surface with sparkling colour. After these first actual experiments with the materials as such, children begin to express their own inner impulses, ones which they may not consciously be aware of or understand, but which release emotional pressures—the phantasies and feelings which they cannot put into words.

No wonder children cannot always name their pictures if we ask them, and the wise adult generally refrains unless it is felt that the boy or girl is longing to talk about his achievements and wants to be asked.

Often he is trying to paint a feeling, an idea or a need, bringing from inside himself in a visual form aspects of how the world appears to him—menacing, frightening, loving, pleasurable or exciting—and his special place in it.

The very skilled adult can sometimes interpret a child's drawings to him and help him to understand the motives that lie behind his pictures of scenes, shapes and figures, but one needs to know both the family background and the child in question very well and the moment, too, when an interpretation of this nature will have some meaning for him.

Just as children play at funerals and weddings so their paintings and drawings may be a reflection of what is happening around them. They can bring a vivid perception, a matter-of-fact reality or compensatory phantasies to the most tragic of events. The children in the concentration camps drew pictures of people going to the gas chambers, truckloads of people arriving and leaving the camps, queues for food, and then some of the happier things they remembered from the past, dreams to console and comfort them and keep their hopes alive even in the most terrible and macabre of situations.[2]

So the very act of being able to put these tragic scenes outside themselves must have made them a little more bearable.

A child's paintings or drawings can also act as a bridge between the world of phantasy and the world of reality. It is, too, a more controlled form of mess than some of the other more primitive materials children use, for paper has certain confining limits. Yet it can, at the same time, act as a safety valve for repressed impulses.

Children use all sorts of shapes, animals, cars, etc., symbolically to represent themselves and their feelings. John's pictures were always full of hate and aggression, guns and bombs, fighting and smashing, hurting, killing and destroying, a never-ending portrayal. Antony drew large and important figures but in the tiny one, tucked away in the corner of his paper, one saw Antony himself, small, insignificant, even unwanted.

Colour in any form always appeals to children and though there is some evidence to suggest that young children use their paints in the order in which the jars with their brushes are placed on the easels this is certainly not always so. In any case, children are not necessarily concerned with the exact colour of the objects or scenes in their paintings. There is no reason, however, why they should not have a good choice of colours and so gradually become aware of the differences between them and the feelings they evoke. Often, it is not the colour but the significance of a particular object that impresses them. Spectacles are often very conspicuously painted; so is a hair ribbon, a pair of boots, anything in fact which appears important and fresh to the child.

There has been a good deal of speculation as to whether the colours children choose are related to their feelings—yellow, green and blue tending to be the happy colours, black and red representing darkness, blood and fire. Perhaps, to a certain extent, this may be true but there are always exceptions, and colours may easily become linked in a child's mind with some special event or experience.

From the purely practical angle paintbrushes of various sizes and paper of different colours, shapes and dimensions should be available. The older child may be able to mix his dry paints in patty-pans and so discover what happens when different colours meet each other. The young child, however, often tends not only to waste his paint but to reduce everything to a dirty, uninspiring grey.

When a painting has been finished, a child may, or may not, want to keep it. Some children, once they have finished a picture, are no longer interested in its future. They have done what they wanted, and that is that. Others treasure their achievements as something to be preserved and taken home to the family.

Finger-painting gives children direct contact between themselves and the actual product they are using. It provides them with a variety of sensations : visual, tactile, kinaesthetic. It is again an acceptable form of mess, and sometimes it is the pleasure in the feel of the paint and its links with bodily interests that are the most important. There is a sweeping freedom about it, an acceptance of its smearing quality, its colour, the way fingers, fists, hands, arms, elbows can be involved which is so pleasurable. Its use can develop into quite controlled movements with older children and patterns with lines, curves, massed colour and pictorial representations can produce most delightful results.

Painting can be either a solitary affair or a friendly social pastime. Children talk to each other and the adult, compare notes, discuss the subject matter in hand, the colours they are using, admire, criticize or comment on their companions' efforts. Older children often enjoy doing a communal painting, each one making his own special contribution.

Another creative material very different in kind from painting yet enabling children to express their feelings and needs in a very visual and concrete way is building with blocks and bricks or other large materials.

Boys and girls can use these things as vehicles for the concepts, wishes, and phantasies that are continually running through their minds. They can invent their own dramatic world, alter it, rebuild it, overthrow it and start all over again. Whether in the playroom, the garden, on the old bomb site, the adventure playground or the countryside, at the play level children become ardent architects and planners as they contrive and construct with any building oddments they can find, while the physical effort involved in moving, lifting, and pushing things gives them a feeling of power over their environment.

Building materials can be explosive in that some children take delight in crashing their edifices to the ground or even hurling their bricks or blocks everywhere. One has to decide how far this explosive behaviour can be allowed and here we are often on the horns of a dilemma.

Margaret Lowenfeld suggests that,

Exercise of the body, of the voice, of the whole person in production of the maximum possible commotion is an absolute necessity at some time or other to every healthy child. Noise is necessary, movement is necessary, and to be healthy these must be allowed to be exactly what they are—shapeless explosions of overplus of energy. . . . Risk and danger are normal elements of adult life, and the ability to cope with dan-

gerous situations is a mark of successful adult character. Every
child has a hunger to emulate in this way the adults who
surround him, and every child, if left to itself, will create games
in which the element of risk appears. [Such play is] the bridge
between the helplessness of childhood and the possession of
power and skill for which he longs.[3]

One cannot, of course, keep children in swaddling clothes and
yet one must guard them against dangers whose possibilities are
quite beyond their understanding. So the possible explosive
quality in building materials and blocks and bricks has to be
considered in relation both to themselves and the other
children.

No mountains would be climbed, seas sailed on, or skies ex-
plored if children's first phantasies of adventure, of power, glory,
achievement and challenge were left unsatisfied.

The world of the city and the town offers children very little
legitimate excitement and so as they get older they often do things
that horrify and anger the adult who sees only anti-social behaviour, destructiveness and aggression in their efforts to court
danger and prove their manhood. Yet building does offer to the
young child a good deal of what he needs in the way of constructive effort and dramatic working out of his desire for power and
excitement.

Children who achieve very little with other materials may find
it easy to pile bricks on each other to really build something; their
sense of achievement grows and they can either play alone or invite others to join them.

With large outdoor equipment, planks, big boxes, trestles,
ladders, etc., an imposing world can be created and children can
climb, balance, jump, crawl and walk on or round the objects
they have built. They often find they need the help of each other
in pushing, pulling or lifting bricks and blocks or other heavy
material, and to experience the breathless pleasure of making these
inanimate objects obey them is very satisfying.

It is unfortunate that in this country really large wooden bricks
are expensive and difficult to get. In the United States and Aus-
tralia where wood is plentiful hollow bricks as large as house
bricks are generally available in plenty. This means that children

can really build a little place big enough and high enough to hide themselves away in when they wish.

Here, if children are to build something of this nature, they need big boxes which often take up a great deal of space or materials other than bricks or boxes : blankets, perhaps, to drape over tables or supports of some kind, bushes in the garden, bracken on the common that can be turned into a hiding place, a tent, a gang hut, or a house in the trees.

Children need to hide themselves away, sometimes, to play their own secret and forbidden games away from the prying eyes and interference of adults and sex play between boys and girls which would no doubt be disapproved of can be indulged in. These sorts of activities are normal, natural and to be expected among young children, and if we look back on our own childhood we may remember some of the secret games we played but which we never mentioned to the grownups for fear of punishment.

Frank Baines in his autobiography *Look Towards the Sea* gives a wonderful account of his first secret sexual experiences when at the age of about five he went to kindergarten and met Althea.

> She taught me a lot. I don't think any other woman taught me more. Refinements, yes, but not facts. We plighted our troth, became sweethearts and intended to marry when we grew up. . . . Opportunities are never lacking for making love, particularly to very young children, for whom the supervisory capacities of grownups rarely embraces sex. 'The dear things are just playing.' Well Althea and I certainly did that.
> . . . Of course I was unfaithful. . . . This time it was a redhead with freckles. . . . On dancing days children could lunch at the school. After lunch they were left to themselves for an hour. . . . We retired to our classroom and spent the hour on the floor underneath the teacher's desk—a peach of a place. Nobody suspected; we were such little dears.[4]

We all need privacy and children especially need these secret places often, in the crowded life of today, difficult to find. Apart from these forbidden pleasures, the building of a little house provides a delightful place for home play, and girls in particular collect all sorts of enchanting impedimenta to deck them out like real homes.

One of the most intriguing parts of Barrie's *Peter Pan* is the little house under the ground. Comfort within and, to make it more real, danger without from the pirates. Here Peter and Wendy were able to behave like a staid, long-married couple and children can identify themselves with these satisfying phantasies.

Boys and girls love getting into small places like cupboards, often shutting themselves in. This has its hazards; sometimes they suddenly become frightened or, if the place is small and airless, suffocate if doors stick and will not open. Perhaps this shutting in, in some small confined place, unconsciously gives children the feeling that they are back in the everlasting security and darkness of the womb.

Waste material of all kinds can be used by children, not perhaps for actual building with, although young children enjoy piling large cardboard boxes on top of each other or sitting inside them, but for making models; and the seven- and eight-year-olds may enjoy working together over some communal effort. This will not be adult-orientated but thought about and discussed by the children themselves. Obviously the adult may help with suggestions and materials if the children get stuck and with the provision of books if these are needed for children to consult.

A tremendous amount of learning goes on concerning the nature and behaviour of objects in the environment. Children discover concepts of large and small, wide and narrow, thick and thin. Weight, i.e. heavy and light, becomes very real to them as they handle different-sized blocks in their constructional play. Things feel different; wood, planks, trestles, all have their own peculiar points of contact.

They discover that the tower of bricks built on an unsteady base falls to the ground, and when a really large construction is made, if children are going to walk on it or use it in other ways, it is useless if it collapses at the slightest touch. They may learn when they are playing with their bricks the action of levers and pulleys and they find it easier to put blocks in a cart than to drag them along on the ground.

Balancing a plank or fitting their bridges safely together needs accurate planning and objects need to be counted and observed for size to see how many and what sort are needed.

All kinds of extra objects can add to the pleasures of bricks and blocks, and little cars, figures, traffic signs, etc., can create a miniature world for children. This may give the adult an insight into how all this appears to the child and the quality and the kind of world he inhabits.

Deprived of this sort of play children cannot gain the concrete knowledge they need. It would have to be learnt through words and pictures and these would mean little, for it is the actual handling, examining and manipulating of objects that is so important to the young.

The adult can help by the sort of materials provided and the space that is available for the bricks and blocks so that children do not feel confined and restricted in their play.

Some children may appear to lack ideas, and the slow and educationally sub-normal child may lack skill of hand and eye co-ordination and so find the frustration of the way actual materials behave when the paste won't stick or the wheels fall off more difficult to bear.

Some children will need more encouragement and cossetting than others. Some adults do so much themselves in order that the finished article should look presentable that children feel discouraged, give up trying and just stand back and watch.

Whether children are using paint, bricks, or in fact any creative materials, it is their enjoyment and interest that is important. Although we should not stand back and let them make a complete mess of something when a suggestion from us would prevent real disappointment and failure, it is their creative efforts that really matter.

7

Learning through play

The world is so full of a number of things
I'm sure we should all be as happy as kings.

ROBERT LOUIS STEVENSON

How do children learn? Certainly they must be mature enough
to be able to accomplish the particular task they are attempting
or that is being imparted to them, and maturation decides the
moment when this becomes possible. To attempt to teach a child
something before he is ready causes endless heartache and disappointment when by simply waiting until he is mature enough
the same skill can often be acquired in a very short time. Learning is an extremely complex process about which there is still
much to discover and here it is perhaps necessary only to refer
very briefly to two of the theories.

One school of thought suggests that active learning attempts
to give meaning to experiences which leave some kind of path in
the brain. The same experiences or similar ones repeated are
reminders of what happened before. The other school feels that
bonds of association and the stamping in of these associations by
constant repetition are what is needed.

As far as young children are concerned, however, we know that
it is play that is the motivating force in their intellectual learning,
and its significance is revealed in every aspect of their development. Obviously, the more intelligent a child is the more he will
learn from his play and the more easily he will be able to spot
the relationship between objects and ideas and apply them to
fresh situations.

Children learn by repetition in that they will practise a new skill in their play with pleasure and zest until they can accomplish it more easily. They will also repeat a satisfying experience rather than one that has proved disappointing and unsuccessful. We all learn from our successes rather than from our continued failures.

The idea of reinforcing what a child learns by some kind of reward—stars, marks or sweets for good work or behaviour—is considered useful by some people. The idea of rewarding children's spontaneous self-chosen play, however, does appear quite ridiculous and pointless.

Emotion is a very important factor both in learning and in play. The older child may grow to hate a particular lesson if he is afraid of the teacher who is mean, overstrict and unkind, and it is very sad to discover the number of adults who were 'put off' a subject in this way.

Young children obviously need a secure setting with loving and understanding adults if they are to get the maximum amount of enjoyment and intellectual stimulation from their play and just 'minding young children' is not enough.

There is, of course, a developmental sequence in children's play and one has only to watch the one-year-old baby and the four-year-old child to see how much progress has been made in three years.

Gesell gives us some very useful behaviour profiles showing us the various play stages through which a child progresses and although children are individuals and therefore vary in what they are able to do there are certain general patterns and landmarks that appear. What interests us here, however, in children's play is how much it is providing them with the foundations on which all their future learning will be built, their ability to communicate and their relationships with others.

One of the first things a child needs to discover and manage is the world around him. Therefore he must explore it physically, for to a young child life is movement. So active play involves running, throwing, jumping and climbing. Children learn to guide a wagon or tricycle down a path or between other children. They push and pull, crawl and balance. In the day-to-day life of play they turn on taps to fetch water, fasten dolls' clothes or move furniture, planks, etc., to make a ship or a playhouse.

In discovering the nature of the physical world mathematical concepts of all kinds are learnt in a practical way. Children handle bricks and pieces of wood of various shapes, sizes and weights that feel and behave differently. They often learn the names and colours of the shapes they are using. They experience the force of gravity, speed, acceleration and momentum, and how a cart will behave if it is let go at the top of a hill.

Children experiment with volume and the way things behave in liquids through their water play; they watch food being cooked in the kitchen, the rice expanding, the water boiling in the kettle for tea; they compare and contrast the different ways in which things react. Experiments with sound, heat, light, magnetism are exciting and the adult needs not only to answer their questions but also to supply explanations and information that are within their understanding.

All sorts of quite ordinary things happen which provide children with number experiences. Perhaps they are asked to fetch two chairs, set the doll's tea party for six, or attach four wheels to the cart they are making.

At the moment most children are intensely interested in the sky, particularly the moon, and even the under-fives have watched the TV programmes of the spaceships and the spacemen, asking countless questions about it all.

This interest has led to all kinds of imaginative and creative play. Because children do not possess the requisite experience and knowledge to understand what is involved and because they enjoy their dramatic play so much they slip quite easily from the world of reality when they ask their questions and want the facts, into the world of phantasy where they can find an imaginative solution to their difficulties, so the impossible becomes possible. 'It's just a case of practice', as the Red Queen remarked, 'Why sometimes I've believed as many as six impossible things before breakfast.'[1]

The world of living and growing things is a constant source of wonder and surprise. Children pick with delight bunches of dusty daisies, lift up stones to discover what is underneath, collect leaves, pebbles, acorns, in fact anything they find which can be carried home from a walk. They sow seeds, plant bulbs, arrange flowers, make little gardens, and they are not as a rule frightened of worms, spiders, etc. if we have not implanted the idea in their heads by our own foolish behaviour.

Richard Church gives us a wonderful picture of his excitement in his early contact with earth, leaves and branches in his play.

> Near the park seat, I squatted behind it, on the border of the loose soil of the horse-riding track, lost in my pleasure at being able to scoop up this element of earth in my hands, and to let it trickle away, grain by grain, here and there an atom of it sparkling, so that I crowed with delight and crooked my fingers like a miser round the treasure. Repeated visits to the park piled experience upon experience, adding to my wisdom, making me more resourceful in exploiting the wonders. I would pluck leaves from bushes and the branches of trees so wide and laden that they reached to the ground. I would read those leaves like a book seeing hieroglyphics where my finger-nails had bruised the surface into darker green lines and shapes.[2]

The weather, too, a favourite topic of conversation with adults, has its own joys, and snow in particular is an exciting material to build with. Boys and girls often want to keep it and bring it indoors in handfuls only to discover that it disappears, leaving a pool of water behind. They see frost patterns on the window, listen to a thunder storm, watch the magic of the rainbow, and wonder about all these strange and mysterious things.

Contacts with birds, animals, etc., either on country walks, on visits to farms or by keeping pets at home or at school can give children a great deal of pleasure.

City children so often believe that milk comes out of a bottle or a fridge—they just don't relate it to a cow. If they live in blocks of flats, pets are often forbidden; although one has no wish to encourage the keeping of birds or animals that are not properly looked after, a child who knows the joy of having something alive to watch, protect and help care for is in possession of something rather special. Animals, too, can sometimes help the disturbed or unhappy child who finds relationships with other children difficult in that it may bridge the gap between the two.

Animals also help children in their first early questions about sex if the cat, for example, has kittens or the dog puppies or they see baby animals on a farm with their mothers.

We know that children in phantasy play out many of the things they do not understand or are anxious about or afraid of, and this is of great value to them, certainly as they play about sex and babies. They do, however, want to know where babies come from and what mothers and fathers do in bed. Because there is a good deal of emotion attached to sex and sexual taboos, it has become a subject often fraught with anxieties and feelings of guilt, and parents do not always find it easy to talk about and explain.

Children may certainly enjoy playing out their birth phantasies but they do want factual information as well and it is less difficult to give when it is done gradually when children are young, and want only a little information simply told, at a time. Perhaps the new dolls now on the market, with masculine sex organs, may encourage the child who does not ask to do so; if these dolls disturb some people may it not be because of their own embarrassment about sex? Children may well accept these new dolls unquestioningly.

It is not enough, however, to tell children just about animals for they may not always see the relationship between their parents and their dogs and cats.

We have already seen how children learn by watching what goes on in the world around them and by imitating what they see happening. Because through play there is a lessening of stress and feelings of guilt as children dramatize their problems and come to terms with them, so they become freer within themselves to learn. No child can give his mind to intellectual interests and pursuits if he is obsessed by feelings of jealousy, hate, aggression and despair. As he learns to manage his world through his play his own feelings of well-being and security are stabilized. Language enables him to verbalize his feelings and phantasies; good relationships with children and adults develop through his play and help him to discover and expand his own individual personality.

It may seem a contradiction in terms to say that a child gains a work attitude through his play but this is one of the things that actually happens.

Children very soon discover that persistence and concentration are needed if a desired end is to be reached and without these qualities little will be accomplished in their play. They will spend long periods in building, painting, constructing, and in phantasy and dramatic play. They will practise a new skill endlessly, they will struggle with heavy equipment and employ endless patience and determination if they really want to accomplish something.

A prerequisite of learning to read is not only concentration and persistence which cannot be taught just on demand, but children must have learnt to recognize different shapes through their play with bricks, puzzles, waste material, etc., to distinguish sounds and to associate them with symbols—a skill closely linked with music and dramatic play of all kinds. They must be able to express themselves in language by talking and communicating with other children and adults, for reading is valueless if children simply learn words, parrot fashion, that mean absolutely nothing to them.

In their painting and drawing they will have made a great many marks on paper—a very necessary requirement when they begin to write.

Children's play involves the solving of problems and the making of decisions and this is very obvious when one watches them. They solve them practically by doing or they solve them by discussion with other children or adults; sometimes they just talk aloud to themselves or anyone near at hand, putting their queries into words to clarify them for themselves or they seek help by going to books and pictures.

If children's reasoning fails it is often the result of lack of knowledge and experience. When John,[3] aged four, was taken to the British Museum with his siblings who insisted on seeing the 'mummies', no one thought he really noticed or questioned their blackened bodies lying in their mummy cases. He had obviously, however, thought about it a good deal. That night when he and his sister were playing in the bath together he noticed that she had got much browner in the sun than he had and, with evident relief in his voice, he told her she was much nearer to dying than he was and that Alec down the road, a little West Indian boy, was even nearer to dying than she and would probably soon be dead. He had been reasoning this out while in the bath playing and thinking back to the mummies he had seen in the Museum.

He came to the wrong conclusions through lack of knowledge and experience.

Lucy at seven was terribly disappointed when her friend Emma was unable to come to tea and play with her. Then, in thinking it out, she reasoned she must find some way to assuage her loneliness; what should she do to solve this problem? So she made a friend by stuffing a large pillow with rags, making a mask for a face, fixing a blond wig for hair and a draught-excluder for arms. The friend proved most comforting, took her place at the tea-table, and was played with for the rest of the day.[4]

So phantasy play was used quite consciously by Lucy to solve a temporary personal problem.·

Whatever we do we must never destroy children's delight and curiosity about the world of people and things and like Mallory the mountaineer they must want to find out about it all because 'it is there'.

Helping young children to learn: The provision of a rich, varied, challenging and interesting environment.
Remembering that :
Factual information should be accurate and given in a way that a child can understand.
Questions should be answered and information supplied. Sometimes a question can be thrown back to a child to see if he can discover the solution for himself.
Correct names should be given for objects and things. Children should be encouraged to observe and learn from their own observations. Opportunities should be provided for active participation in what is going on.
Children should be talked to in sentences; single words are not enough. Without in any way upsetting a child the wrong use of words can be corrected. When Sidney said of a duck that he was opening his mouth the adult was able to say he was opening his bill.
Children's attention can be drawn to new objects and experiences.
Expeditions to places of interest, a market, post office, railway station, etc., provide endless material for talk and dramatic play.
Books and pictures should be available for children to look at and

enjoy; stories should be told and read to them. Objects of all kinds can be shown to children for them to look at, handle, use, and talk about. Suggestions for making a play activity more valuable and interesting can sometimes be made when children have reached the end of their own ideas.

Children's natural desire to discover how things work should be encouraged. Help should be given to a child when by so doing he can turn his failure into a success.

A particular skill should be taught or explained to a child if he needs it or wants it.

Understandable and sensible reasons should be given if a child is forbidden or prevented from doing something he wishes to do.

Children's 'why' questions, even if they deal with things he has been told he cannot do, should be answered with understanding and good sense.

Praise, encouragement, thanks, appreciation and affection should be used generously in contacts with children. Kind, generous and cooperative behaviour should be approved of and encouraged; unkind, spiteful, bullying and anti-social behaviour should be gently but firmly discouraged. Simple play rules such as : no throwing sand in the sand pit, no pushing on heights, etc., should be explained to children and adhered to.

If there is a disabled or seriously disturbed child his difficulties should be explained very simply to the other children so that their warm and protective feelings are aroused rather than their hostile and critical ones.

The acquiring of acceptable social skills by a shy and awkward child should be encouraged and help given so that he becomes a member of the group instead of remaining an outsider.

Adults should set an example by their own understanding, warm, loving and generous impulses.

PART TWO

How children play

8

Observations of house play

Children reveal themselves most transparently in their play life. They play not from outer compulsion but from inner necessity.

ARNOLD GESELL, *The Child from Five to Ten*

The adult who is unfamiliar with the way or even the significance of children's play, may not recognize it even when it is going on. Healthy children, of course, are always doing something. Seen in the streets, in buses, shopping with their parents, they are not as a rule idle; they may be bored but they will be on the lookout for something to do all the time. It may be something seemingly very simple, but children are often able to bring to what they are doing the diversity and richness of their own imaginations, their sense of drama or their need to discover and explore.

In reading the observations[1] on home play (and one sees this in the other observations too) one gets a bird's eye view of a complex activity and one is struck by the amazing ability children have of combining the world of make-believe and the world of reality.

Here, for example, in the observations their imaginations are at work recreating aspects of adult living, the things they have watched and heard going on around them.

Added to this the whole scenes are coloured by the freshness with which they see things which to us are no longer clothed with 'celestial light' but are jobs to be done, or obstacles to be overcome as quickly as possible. They have an extraordinary capacity of sliding one incident into another; make-believe play overlaps and changes in the twinkling of an eye. Here in these observations one can see these things happening.

House Play

1

John is in the bedroom area of the house. He winds up the alarm clock 'So we'll know when it's time to get up,' he says. Ellen strips all the dolls' cradles. She puts the covers in a heap on the floor, then says in a shocked voice, 'Look what that naughty girl has done! Look what she's done.' She scolds continuously as she replaces the covers on the cradles. She suddenly catches sight of John, who is crouching on the floor looking for the clock-winder which has fallen off. Ellen remarks excitedly 'I know, you be my pussy-cat! Miau!' John responds with several miaus; he has become a cat.

Ellen brings John into the kitchen area of the house but he stops halfway to crawl around the bedroom where there is more space. Several other children are sitting round the table. Ellen remarks loudly that her pussy-cat was coming to school as John is still on the floor miauing loudly.

Ellen hurries out to the book corner and gets two books. John gets up off the floor and looks at his book. He has stopped being a pussy-cat for the moment.

Ellen suddenly takes the books away, pushes John down on the floor and says, 'Go on, now, you're going to be my pussy-cat and I'm going to put a nurse's uniform on.'

John becomes a pussy-cat again and, jumping into the large bed in the house, pulls the blanket over him. Ellen suddenly sees he is sucking the blanket. She rushes over and wrenches it out of his mouth saying, 'Don't tear that or I'll hit you, pussy-cat.'

Dawn, another child, comes into the house and Ellen says, 'That's my cat. He's got to stay in here, he's ill. It's cold in here today and he has got to stay in bed.' The pussy cat now turns into a baby. He sucks his thumb, and makes infantile noises. Ellen says comfortingly, 'Don't cry, baby, Nursie will look after you.'

2

Four boys are sitting round the table in the home corner. The table is laid for tea but the boys are taking no interest in this. They each have a gun made from 'Makimor'. Each gun is of a different design and at intervals the boys get up, rush over and collect some more bits to add to their firearms.

Adrian wants to play with the tea-things and he hovers near. Eventually grabbing a tea-pot from the stove, he attempts to pour out tea for the boys, but they are not interested. He takes a cup and saucer, puts them on the floor and pours out tea for himself. He keeps a wary eye on the boys as though he is waiting for a chance to sit at the table. He fetches a saucepan from the stove and tries to give the boys some dinner, but they are still much too preoccupied with their guns. They are not playing as a group; each boy is interested in himself, and there is no conversation.

Three of the boys get up and go; one, Andrew stays behind. He collects all the saucepans, etc., pushes them into the oven with a great clatter, closes the door and rushes off. Adrian puts the tea-pot and kettle into a small truck, saying to no one in particular, 'I won't be long.'

Sharon appears, looking very officious and determined. She has an air of righteous indignation; she rescues the tea-pot and kettle from Adrian and puts them away in their right place. Stephen, who has just come in and has been messing about with the oven door, is pushed aside, quite gently, by Sharon, who closes the door most efficiently.

Beverley comes in and sits down at the table as if waiting for something.

Sharon bustles back. She tidies the cloth and says to the passive Beverley: 'Now I'm the mummy and you can be my little girl.' She then rushes away because she sees out of the corner of her eye the boys, who still have their guns but are congregating round the ironing board. It is really quite by accident that they have gathered there.

Sharon explains hastily, 'Don't you do my ironing. Leave my ironing alone.' (No one is touching it.) She puts up a clothes-horse, and as she does so she catches sight of a plastic milk-bottle on the floor. 'Oh, I must get some milk for my baby.' Beverley goes over to the telephone (there are two on a nearby shelf) and says, 'Hello, nurse.'

Sharon looks at Beverley and listens to her conversation, then puts the baby into the cot and tucks it up, tidying the covers in a very efficient way.

Adrian comes over and tries to use the other telephone. Sharon calls out, 'No, don't, it's mine.' Adrian tries the one that Beverley has just left, but Sharon says 'It's Beverley's.'

Adrian grabs a bottle from the table. Sharon pounces on him saying, 'No, I need it, I need it.'

Adrian says, 'So do I.' Sharon says quietly, 'Oh, all right, you can have it.'

Seven-year-olds

3

Three girls and a boy, all dressed up, are playing in the home corner. Ann is saying to the others, 'We've got heaps of parcels.' Babs says, 'Ann is getting married.' Cliff asks what is in the parcels and Babs says sweets.

Ann remarks that she is going on her honeymoon and asks who will be her bridesmaid.

There is a huddle of the children whispering together. Finally Ann breaks away and takes Clifford's arm, saying, 'This is the bridegroom. Do you take this woman?' Then she says to Dora, 'No, you be the preacher.' Dora asks what she has to say. Ann repeats the sentence 'Do you take this woman to be your lawful wedded wife?' but Dora can't remember it. Babs says, 'Let me say it,' and Dora in a huff says 'I won't play' and goes off.

Cliff says, 'Hurry up, I want to get married.' Babs says, 'Tell me what to say.' Ann repeats again, 'Do you take this man to be your lawful wedded husband?' Babs stumbles over the words and Ann, thoroughly impatient sweeps off, dragging her bridegroom with her.

Ann and Clifford quickly return and there is talk about the presents. Clifford suddenly says: 'Let's pretend it's Christmas morning. I've got lots of presents for you.'

Ann sits down and pretends to open the presents.

There is now a sudden reversal of rôles. Ann becomes the mother and Clifford her baby. Ann offers her baby food. Then as Clifford departs there is another quick change as Ann calls out: 'Bye-bye, Dad.'

The play ends as the children are called to clear up.[2]

4

*Four boys in the home corner make themselves into male and
female personalities. One dresses himself up as a mother, one as
a little girl, while the other two boys stay as they are. They argue
and fuss about the play and who should do what for some
minutes. Then one of the boys calls out that dinner is ready. Alan
says, 'Nice roast potatoes.' Then he and Colin argue as to which
of them is the father. Alan suggests that Colin is the grandfather:
'That's still a man.' Alan then says he'll be telling the time so
they can pretend it's tea time.*

*The boys who are dressed as a mother and a little girl have by
this time vanished; obviously they are tired of not knowing what
is really happening.*

*Colin calls to two nearby girls, 'Come and play and be mother
and auntie,' but the girls refuse. The play then completely disintegrates and the boys run off.*

In observing these home corner plays one can see how at one
moment John (observation 1) is a little boy winding a clock in
order that he will know, as he says, 'When to get up,' which probably implies a number of ideas about getting up and universal
time in general which he could not possibly explain and which
he has strange, vague ideas about anyway; while the next,
at Ellen's suggestion, he has turned himself into a cat crawling
and miauing about the floor. This transformation into an animal
happens more than once even in this short play. He slips in and
out of the cat and human world with the greatest of ease and all
he needs to do is to crawl on the floor and miau.

The whole set-up of home corner play with a group of children
offers all sorts of possibilities of imitating the adult world, of playing out scenes and experiences with half-remembered scraps of
conversation suggesting that children observe adults perhaps even
more closely than we observe them.

Nor do they always need the elaboration of a great deal of
material in school. A well-equipped home corner may help to
stimulate imaginative play, but the children's own powers of
make-believe, and their sense of drama, can add without effort
a great deal. When real food is not available there is always 'pre-

tend' food, dolls become babies, and other children take over whatever parts may be assigned to them.

Florence McDowell in telling of her Victorian childhood in County Antrim[3] describes how, 'the little girls played at wee houses, constructing their walls one stone high, and laying out kitchen, parlour and bedroom with careful blanks for doorways. All broken crockery, flat stones and obsolete utensils from the farm house were pressed into service for furnishing their wee houses, and their housewifely instincts were first called into play in thus caring for homes of their own.'

Girls sometimes seem to be surer and more confident in their play of the feminine rôle in the home than boys do in their play as fathers, for one sees them cooking food, tidying the house, looking after the children.

This is because, perhaps, girls are able to see and share imaginatively more easily in what goes on at home and what their mothers do; things they have seen happening so often in real life.

To care for in a kindly fashion, and to organize the home in an efficient way, are things which small girls become aware of early on for, generally speaking, if the mother in the home is either feckless, incapable or too ill physically or mentally to hold the reins of the household confidently in her hands, the family goes to pieces and disintegrates.

C. S. Lewis[4] in his autobiography talks about his own mother and what happened when she died. 'We gradually lost her,' he says, 'as she was gradually withdrawn from our life into the hands of nurses and delirium and morphia, and as our whole existence changed into something alien and menacing, as the house became full of strange smells and midnight noises and sinister whispered conversations. . . . With my mother's death all settled happiness, all that was tranquil and reliable disappeared from my life.'

No wonder small girls watch and identify with this universal provider of love and care.

Boys also want to play at having a home, being fathers and being useful. Adrian (observation 2) obviously wanted to play out some aspect of home life and when he put the tea-kettle and the tea-pot into the cart to wheel them away he may have been trying to combine both rôles. Sharon, however, took them away from him quite firmly and put them back in their places where they belonged, for order must be maintained in the home. However, as we shall see, if the boys appear less sure in the home corner, in their brick play they do feel and act more confidently.

At times the home corner becomes just a place which acts as a background. The boys sitting silently at the table with their guns were not really any part of family play. Perhaps they were merely remembering a vague scene from TV with men sitting round a table in some shanty town with their guns at the ready; so they felt that that is what they should do too.

Activities which in real life children are unable to do—cooking, cleaning, ironing, using the telephone—can all be indulged in, and the telephone in particular is very useful as a means of communication. Children listen to imaginary conversations, laugh, look worried and reply. The doctor can be summoned, father can be talked to, and even the shopping done.

As children take over and change rôles from humans to cats, from mothers to babies, from husbands to fathers (observation 3) in the seven-year-old play, they also become aware of what is considered right or wrong, what is naughty, remembering what they have been told. To get out of bed when commanded to stay there is bad and even as a cat, John must not suck his blanket (observation 1) without threat of punishment.

Yet they can indulge, too, in all sorts of forbidden things: pretend to lick their plates, throw the bedclothes about, chastise their dolls.

To show anger, which children often feel in relation to their parents but which they are obliged to hide and disguise, is possible in home play. The setting is right and with no conscious awareness that this is what is happening, their hostility and aggression are able to find a safe and constructive outlet, either verbally or by dumping the baby in bed, pushing the boys out of the home corner or vigorously dusting or sweeping.

The lightning changes that go on make it difficult sometimes to keep up with or even understand what is happening, particularly if one turns away for a moment. Thus Sharon (observation 2) is suddenly reminded that the baby must be fed when she sees a plastic bottle lying on the floor.

Time means little in dramatic play even to seven-year-olds and the presents that the bride and bridegroom receive (observation 3) quickly became Christmas presents, things much more familiar to most children.

Relationships also alter with great rapidity, partly because to children they often appear easily interchangeable. When Ann's bridegroom (observation 3) is suddenly referred to as 'Dad' she herself may have been a little confused about husbands and fathers and the difference between them.

Boys often feel they really need a mother-figure in their home play and in observation 4 their activities soon disintegrated when no feminine influence was at hand.

Jealousies and rivalries become apparent as dolls are quarrelled over or boys (as sweethearts, dads or husbands) are either desired or rejected. Children emerge as leaders or play quietly on their own, seeming regardless of what is happening around them. Individual phantasies overlap; children use each other as they play or go off quite suddenly to do something else.

Obviously home play is full of drama for both sexes as adult patterns of behaviour are imitated. Obviously, too, many of the unconscious phantasies that children have about their parents and family life in general can be worked through in their play.

The relationships between parents, their quarrels and disagreements, their kindnesses and generosities, are observed and absorbed by children.

Children's own feelings about other members of the family, younger and older siblings, can be expressed; the dolls who take the place of babies often come in for a good deal of rather aggressive treatment. At the same time children lavish quite a lot of loving care on their dolls, cuddling them, crooning to them and tucking them tenderly up in bed. They themselves often enjoy and need the change from being the mother in the play to being the baby who wants looking after and petting, particularly when they need to regress and be small and helpless once again. They find comfort and pleasure in sucking water out of dolls' bottles, perhaps expressing an unconscious desire to return to the safety and comfort of babyhood.

Grandparents appear in children's home play sometimes as warm, stable individuals—'our gran'—or as awkward creatures who tend to complain about noise and manners in general.

A child who has been rejected by his or her parents often shows in either home corner play or play with miniature dolls and furniture a great deal of hate. Patsy, a six-year-old, when playing with a small set of dolls and dolls' furniture, showed consistent hostility and real aggression, particularly towards the mother doll. Both verbally and by her actions she indicated how bitter and angry her feelings towards them were. Some children will turn away from such play as if the memories it evokes are too painful to contemplate.

Some young children deprived of a normal home life, particularly if they have been moved about from one place to another, seem to be in a state of complete uncertainty as to where they belong. Their play tends to be completely unorganized and all they seem able to do is to pile up the dolls' furniture without any link with the small doll family that goes with it, as if a life at home with parents or siblings means nothing at all to them.

9
Clay and painting

1

Three boys are playing with clay. They pummel it, squeeze it, put their fingers round it and pull it. Andrew begins to make a house. He takes great delight in poking his fingers into the lumps and makes three deep holes. He pulls his half-made house to pieces, banging it and changing its shape, pulling and twisting. While he is doing this he appears to be day-dreaming and his eyes wander round the room.

2

A group of children is at the clay table. Ruth rolls, presses and squeezes some small lumps of clay. Colin and Mavis experiment, banging and poking it. Peter and Jimmy are very excited, they bang and pummel large lumps of clay, rolling it and flattening it. None of the children appears at this stage to want to make anything.

3

John takes a large piece of clay and rolls it into a ball in his fingers. He talks all the time. 'My sister, she's got a doll, a new one. I want a gun, my Dad won't buy a gun, he won't buy me one.' He begins to shape his clay into what looks like a weapon. 'It's my birthday, do you know it's my birthday?' he says, looking round at the other children sitting at the clay table. 'It's not your birthday,' says Ellen, rolling out a snake with a long piece of clay. 'It is' shouts John, pounding his fist on the table. 'I'll make a horrid man to eat you, no, I'll make a girl, a horrid girl, who says it's not my birthday and I'll smash her up.' He squeezes his clay fiercely and begins to roll it out. Suddenly Jerry passes, wearing a cowboy hat. John jumps from his chair, drops his clay and starts to chase him. He shouts, 'I'll shoot you so look out.' Both children vanish into the garden.

4

Martin, a difficult six-year-old, is admitted to hospital after a traffic accident. He is very disturbed and unhappy, and unfortunately is badly handled by the nursing staff—they punish and slap him for his uncooperative behaviour.

One day, according to the nursing staff, he has been particularly naughty and he and another boy are separated from the other children who have quite recently had a teacher in to help them in their play.

The observer finds them alone, with nothing to do, and gives them some dough. Martin talks and plays with his material, making a little cup and plate.

Then the nurse and physiotherapist come in. When they have gone, Martin grabs his dough, makes a lump in each hand and bangs them cymbal-wise violently and viciously together shouting, 'Smack, smack, smack, smack,' eight times in all. He then looks at the observer and bursts into tears. He is comforted by being nursed.

Painting. Four to five year-olds

1

Beverley begins with blue paint. She makes a circle and then fills it in. 'Look, my water's blue,' she says. She uses very careful, gentle brush-strokes. 'Now I'm going to use brown. It looks as if it's going to be something out of space.' She adds a speck of black and then makes radiating 'feelers', attached to the blue patch. 'I would think it's a man in bed, my painting is funny.'

2

Kevin takes green paint and makes a square. He adds two green legs, then mixes blue and red paint and adds two more legs. Now he makes a head with two eyes and a mouth and adds two simple horns and what appears to be a beard.

He tackles the activity in a very decisive manner. His strokes are quick and purposeful and he is completely absorbed. He finishes his painting and removes it from the easel.

3

Juliet begins by taking blue paint. She writes her name across the top. Then taking red she makes a face and adds two long strokes to represent hair. 'She's not got any ribbons. I have. Her hair's just hanging down.' Juliet's hair is quite long and tied in two bunches. As she paints she talks to herself. 'Careful . . . so it doesn't drip,' she murmurs. She takes black paint and makes a body, then she chooses blue paint. 'This is her skin.' Taking red paint she adds arms and legs 'I must make arms now; legs now.' This is a running commentary as she works. 'It's a picture of me.' She removes it from the easel and puts it to dry.

4

Tony paints with his left hand. He chooses blue paint first. He makes a circle which he then fills in with vigorous strokes. He takes green paint and makes several lines; the paint begins to drip. He takes blue paint again and makes several lines and obliterates the green; as he does this he uses a strong scrubbing movement.

Tony appears to choose his colours very deliberately; he looks right into the jar before he decides. He now takes black paint and makes thick black strokes on an empty part of the paper. It is a vertical line of great intensity which is made with great concentration. Now Tony chooses yellow paint and makes a similar line, next to, but not quite touching, the black line. He now produces some spots by pressing the brush firmly on to the paper. The paint, however, drips. He scrubs the spots away until these have merged with the central mass of colour.

He is engrossed in his painting, unaware of being watched.

5

Peter is a little boy of $4\frac{1}{2}$ who has been in hospital for three weeks. He has been quiet, well-behaved, docile and obedient to an unnatural degree.

When it is suggested he might like to paint, he says he doesn't know what to draw. He fingers the crayons he has selected. To turn his thought away from the bare cubicle in which he is lying, the observer asks him where he lives. Peter replies almost in tears, 'Oh, it's a long road and buses go past. I have forgotten what it is called.' He is asked what his house is like. Without replying he frantically draws his picture in just under three minutes. Then he says, 'That's my house and the next one, and you walk along that road and when you see that house [pointing to the one in the middle of the picture which is red with a brown roof] that's where my mummy is, and tell her to come and take me home.' Here he bursts into tears and has a good cry on the observer's lap.

6

Anne, aged three and in hospital, asks to paint (and paints were available) the moment her mother says goodbye and leaves her. Her mother comes to see her as often as possible but not every day, and Anne has been in hospital nine weeks.

Although there is a complete range of colours available she chooses black, green and blue and works quickly and rather frantically. As she finishes in one minute flat, she thrusts the material away and says, 'That's my mum' and runs to join in some other play. She appears ready, though this may be too simple a surmise, to give her painting away.

7

Raymond, a boy of seven badly burned on his legs, starts painting saying, 'This is the sky' (painting a strip of blue at the top of the painting); 'This is my house' (painting it with red). After this he says nothing more about his painting, but paints some yellow and red areas in the picture.

Weeks later he suddenly talked about it. He explained that the picture was all about the fire, the fire brigade, the pain and the ambulance. Although up to then he had never spoken of his accident he started telling everyone the gruesome details of his grafting operations. His successive paintings were in themselves usual for a seven-year-old.

Play with clay and dough has already been discussed in relation to the help it gives children to work through some of their feelings of hostility and aggression. The observations here show various kinds of play. In the first two observations the children clearly did not want to make anything definite with their clay or dough. They were far more interested in its feel and consistency; they wanted to squeeze and roll it, pummel and pound it. There is very little clue as to their thoughts while they were doing this as they were not talking; nor did their expressions tell anything.

John was certainly working out some of his hostility and aggression in relation to his feelings, about his father and the gun he wanted. The fact that he transferred his anger on to Ellen may have been because it was safer and easier to hate her, on whom he was not really dependent, than to hate his father who, as a part of his family, was important and necessary to him; and he probably felt less guilty about it all. He did not appear unduly upset and was able to run off for more boisterous and lively play with Jerry.

To Martin it was all much more difficult. His general be-haviour, which the nursing staff had labelled as naughty and uncooperative, must have already disturbed and upset him in his loneliness and fear in the hospital situation; and the fact that he was dealing with it with aggression rather than withdrawal was probably a healthy sign.

The dough, and a warm, friendly adult who, without saying anything, obviously understood how he felt must have com-forted him a little. He was even able to make a cup and plate which, perhaps, unconsciously signified for him something pleasant and satisfying, the receiving of a gift, of love, in fact. Then the sudden appearance of the nurse and the physiothera-pist brought back all his feelings of anger, misery and hatred. His dough became a symbol of his anger; he shouted 'smack' (eight times) as he banged his clay; this is what had been done to him so this is what he would like to do to others. All this feel-ing in this particular situation for a child only six years old and away from home was so overwhelming that he burst into tears.

The same kind of behaviour shows in the crayoning and paint-ing of the children in hospital. Peter (observation 5) was over-whelmed by his misery and despair, though he had been a docile and obedient little boy, hiding his feelings most of the time. When, however, he had been helped to say something in crayon, he could hardly express it for his anxiety and unhappiness; and when he had eventually done his drawing, as fast as he could, as if it were too painful to linger over, he burst into tears.

Raymond, too, put his fears and anxieties into his paintings, and although when he was actually doing his picture he did not say anything, it must have had a releasing effect. Weeks later he became able to talk about it and to tell everyone all about his burns, and his skin-grafts.

Anne, too, painted in a rather frantic way a picture of her 'mum' and perhaps she also felt too disturbed to stay and even contemplate her picture; she ran quickly off to play with something else.

The children in observations 1, 2, 3 and 4 all appeared happy, normal children. They painted with pleasure and concentration, using their colours carefully. Beverley wasn't sure what she was painting until she had finished. Kevin didn't name his painting, but seemed satisfied over the results. Juliet and Tony also enjoyed their efforts.

10

Brick play

1

Angus and Tracy are each building a separate tower quite near each other. They are both singing and making up the words to the tune of 'This Old Man'. Angus keeps trying to finish Tracy's tower by putting a roof on it. They each build another tower. Each tower has a roof. Soon they have four towers in a line, two tall ones and two small ones. David comes along, sits near Tracy and says to her in a confiding way, 'You don't know what my mum's going to have when I get home.' Angus, who is listening intently, says, 'No, what?' David, 'A birthday.' Spontaneously they all begin to sing, 'Happy birthday to you,' and perform a little dance round the wooden towers. Angus says, 'Let's knock it down now, shall we?' Tracy agrees, 'Yes, come on.' However they don't actually knock it down, but pull it to pieces, making the appropriate noises as each block falls. When they are all in a heap the children try to sit on them with loud giggles but find it very uncomfortable. Angus tries to cover himself with the bricks, balancing them on his arms, legs and head; this isn't very success-ful and he leaves the bricks. David, who has been watching, says very quickly to Tracy. 'Let's make a birthday cake, my mum's 32, she's having 32 candles.' Angus returns and he and Tracy put the bricks in a large square and stand several of them up-right in the middle to represent candles. David watches them closely. The children all begin to sing, 'Happy birthday to you', again. They then carefully blow out the candles. When this is done they pull the birthday cake to pieces and go off to play somewhere else.

2

Norman gets out the large, hollow bricks. 'I'm going to make a road, the road to Hammerley. I'm making a big road. This is the corner. What I need is some more cars.' He goes to fetch some. Thoughtfully, he says, 'If a car goes over the road it doesn't matter,' and he demonstrates by running it over the edge of the blocks. He collects a small narrow plank and tries to balance it on a small block; it looks rather like a see-saw. 'This is going to be a bridge,' he remarks. 'It's going to be a high, high bridge because I like bridges.'

He chooses a car from his collection. 'This is my car, I put bread in this van, it's a van-car.' He pushes the car along the road making car noises. 'Now some more bricks, it's got to be higher still, like this,' and he looks at the observer and raises his arms to indicate height.

A beautiful, wooden working model of a crane is available and Norman makes use of this. He sits on it and propels himself along on his feet. He experiments with the various handles and levers, and sees how the arm of the crane can be lowered and raised. He hooks a large block on to the rope. 'Look, this is dangerous.' He carefully hauls the block up. He now sits on the seat of the crane, making appropriate noises. He steers the crane to the shelves on which the blocks are.

Suddenly, the ratchet on the jib slips and the arm falls to its lowest position. Norman looks rather alarmed. 'Look! What shall we do? You'll have to do something!' (This is an appeal to the observer.) On being told to raise the top lever, he follows the direction and seems relieved to see that he is able to repair the damage for himself. He leaves the crane, saying he is going to play with the trains. He begins to lay out the rails with bricks and fetches a small engine. He says to the observer, 'Don't worry, you needn't move. I'll make the rails go round you and if the train does run over you the crane will lift it off and then you'll be all right.' As he is finishing his rails, four girls come over to the nearby stand where the dressing up clothes are. Norman watches them. 'They can choose anything they want, can't they?' he says somewhat wistfully. 'I'm a boy, aren't I? Could a boy wear the ambulance clothes?' (He probably means the nurses' aprons which are hanging up there.) He watches the girls putting on frilly skirts and fancy hats, heaves a deep sigh and silently returns to his trains.

3

Grant is balancing one block on top of another. He looks at an adult who is standing near and says, 'Good, isn't it?' He smiles. He keeps trying out this feat several times. He walks a few yards, turn round and then walks back before the block drops. 'Careful, careful,' he keeps saying to himself.

He looks at the blocks he has got and begins to count them to himself, one, two, three. Someone distracts his attention for a moment and he says rather quietly, 'Now where was I?' He had lost track of his counting. He starts again. 'One, two, three, four, this number five is a heavy one,' and he stoops and picks up one of the bricks, pretending that it is so very heavy that he can hardly lift it. He goes on talking very quietly to himself, absorbed in what he is doing.

4

Mike and Bruce place a wooden slide between two box-like frames about two feet from the ground. Mike tells Bruce to get some more boxes and Bruce goes off. Janice comes over to watch, but Mike raises his arm menacingly and shouts, 'Go away, you can't come here.' The two boys build a wall on the far side of their structure, using 20 big boxes. Mike climbs to the top of what he now calls a ship and fixes a large electric cable on to a trestle which Bruce drags between the frame and the screen. Bruce sits on the trestle, takes the wheel and pretends to drive the car.

Climbing along the centre structure Mike shouts, 'Get on board, we leave in six minutes.' Bruce climbs on to the ship, David joins them, Mike shouts, 'Even if you pull the brake, you're away from the shore. You'll have to walk down. We won't stop the ship. Now what shall we have to eat?' They pretend to eat. Mike shouts, 'Ship ahoy! Ship ahoy!'. David says, 'Ship ahoy! means get started.' Mike shouts, 'Ship ahoy!' and pretends to blow a trumpet as he stands in the middle of the ship.

Mike goes over to a large see-saw and laboriously pulls it near to the ship.

'That's the filler,' says David. 'It fills the boat up with petrol. Some ships sink. If they have one funnel they have one oil tank.' Both boys pretend to fill the tank in the middle of the ship.

At this moment a young helper comes over and says, 'Will you take me to London?'

Mike shouts, 'Get off. No one is allowed on this boat and filler but us.' Leaning towards her he says, 'You're not allowed in here. You know why? It's full of olive oil and it's all over the place.' The young helper then takes a plank from the ship. Mike shouts 'Don't do that, don't touch it.' The helper says 'I'm only taking it to make the little ones a see-saw.' Bruce shouts back 'Put it where you found it, you beastie,' and starts to cry. The young helper remarks that they shouldn't be silly and she will put it back soon. 'Put it back now, you beast,' shouts Mike. The helper puts it back while the boys scowl angrily and mutter among themselves.

David says, pointing to the retreating helper, 'She says we can't have any more boxes. She's horrible. She says we might shoot everybody.' Mike shrugs his shoulders. 'She's only pretending, don't take any notice, just go and get some more boxes.'

At this point Paul joins the group, carrying an oilcan filled with water. David says, 'This is the filler, it has to go each time back to the harbour to get filled up with oil.' He points to Paul's oil saying, 'Press it here and stop when it starts filling up. Press the button. Press it quickly.' David shows Paul where to press the imaginery button and Paul holds the can in place, regulating the supposed flow of oil.

Mike suddenly starts shouting:

> 'Rock around the clock,
> One o'clock, two o'clock, three o'clock,
> Four o'clock, five o'clock, six o'clock rock,
> Rock, rock around the clock.'

All the boys chase each round the ship. David shouts, 'There's a real fire, into the ship and sail away, get the fire brigade, get the fire brigade.'

Mike says, 'Stop singing that and get the fire brigade, I'll press the fire-bell and the fire brigade will come.'

Gavin, who has joined the play, says, 'He told me he could smell something. He told me he could smell smoke.'

Mike says to David, 'Don't start singing again, press the fire bell.' Gavin then remarks he wishes he was in hospital as there is a real button there and if you press it the real fire brigade will come.

Mike sings his song again loudly and shouts 'Press the button.'

The teacher then explains to them that you have to break the glass in front of the button before you can press it.

All the boys scream to make a ringing noise and leap off the ship, falling in a heap on the floor.

A good deal more noisy play goes on. The boys move to a fort they have built previously, calling out that they are robbers and pirates. Gavin picks up a piece of paper off the floor and breaks off small pieces, saying, as he hands them round to several children, that whoever gets a piece can come to his birthday.

At this point the children are called in to get ready for their lunch.

5

Alan is using the large, hollow, coloured blocks. He is building a tower. 'Look at my building,' he shouts. He topples it over and claps his hands excitedly. 'Do it again, I'd better.' He sings a la-la-ing song as he builds.

He places the blocks very gently and carefully; the tower almost topples. He watches it from the corner of his eye while he goes to fetch a block. He is just steadying the tower when an adult calls out, 'That's high enough, topple it the other way.'

Alan makes the blocks fall, but his enjoyment seems to have vanished.

6

Julian and Pete are in the corner of the playroom with a large pile of bricks strewn round them. Pete is shy, quiet and retiring and has only just begun to make contacts with the other children. Together, without talking, they sort out the bricks and begin to build. Pete puts four large bricks together, gets on them and jumps off, a look of excitement on his face. Julian looks on in a slightly condescending way, as if this is kids' stuff to him.

Pete gets more bricks and begins to make a high platform. Julian starts to lay bricks round Pete's mounting edifice, then fetches some little cars and moves them round, making the appropriate sounds.

Pete gets more excited as his platform gets higher. He finds he cannot get on to it easily, so he fetches a chair, then triumphantly mounts, waves his arms and shouts to no one in particular, 'Look at me, look at me.' Bill, casually, passing, snaffles his chair. Pete screams out in a scared way, 'My chair, I want my chair.' He scrambles off his structure and rushes away leaving Julian to play alone.

7

Paul and Adam come to the block corner each wearing a cowboy hat. Adam says, 'Shall we play forts?' and Paul says, 'Yes, let's.' 'This is how a fort goes,' says Adam and together they move the blocks until they are in the wanted position.

Paul says, 'I'll go and get my gun, the fort's nearly done.' He goes and fetches a long narrow block and Adam says to a passing adult, 'We aren't playing cowboys any more, we're playing cavalries.'

Adam says to Paul, 'Are you ready, Bill?' 'Yes, ready, Bill' Paul replies. The two boys begin to knock down the fort.

Then they begin to rebuild it but this time it becomes a sort of hidey hole and they lie on the floor, each having a gun which he pushes through the gaps in the bricks. Adam shouts 'We're shooting the cowboys! We're cavalries, aren't we?' Suddenly he jumps to his feet.

'On your marks,' he shouts. 'On your marks, get set, march.' They both march round the room, guns on their shoulders.

8

Alice sits alone among the bricks singing to herself. Then she builds a circle of flat bricks round herself so that she is shut in. She sings quietly, 'Oh my baby, baby, baby,' then looks dreamily about, seeming oblivious of the noise and bustle in the room.

The other children pass and repass. David comes by and offers Alice a sweet which she takes in a dreamy fashion. Then quite suddenly she jumps up, pushes her bricks aside and, going over to the painting easel, picks up a brush and begins to paint.

Bricks or blocks are a stimulating play material which children enjoy for a variety of reasons. Several of them sang or hummed to themselves during their play (observation 4) and bricks lend themselves to solitary play as well as cooperative efforts.

Norman and Alan (observations 2 and 4) both enjoy making something on their own without help from anyone. Bricks can change into anything a child wants and David (observation 1) seems to be obsessed by the thought of his mother's birthday; he has to talk about it and tell the other children all the interesting details. They give him just the sort of kindly encouragement he needs and the bricks are turned into candles on a birthday cake and the children obligingly sing, 'Happy birthday to you'.

Pete (observation 5) wants to feel big and important and by building his bricks into a high platform he is able to get on top of them and feel proud. Grant (observation 3) also gets a feeling of achievement about what he is making; he obviously thinks it was good and feels happy and satisfied with what he is doing.

Mike and Bruce playing together built an elaborate ship (observation 3). All sorts of phantasy were involved. David joins them, pulling over a large see-saw to act as a filler which will fill the ship up with petrol. Quite a lot of strenuous work went into the moving of the see-saw. The boys obviously did not want anyone to interfere with their play; Janice was told to go away and the boys built a wall to keep intruders out.

The young helper who unfortunately interfered with their play thoroughly upset them and there was some verbal aggression when they shouted at her and called her names. David was quite upset when he said she had told them they could not have any more boxes. Mike took it more philosophically, telling David to take no notice of her. Bruce who had also used verbal aggression and called the helper a beast, was upset enough to cry; perhaps he also felt a little guilty about calling her names.

Suddenly there was all the excitement of deciding, for no special reason, to call the fire brigade and Gavin, who had joined in the play, appeared almost to believe that someone had smelt smoke. Mike had been singing to himself during the play, but was very firm with David who, he felt, was talking too much about calling the fire brigade but doing nothing positive about it. Pressing a bell was demanded several times and this reminded Gavin of hospital bells. Pressing things had come into the play before when the oil can had to be pressed.

At this stage a passing adult explained that you had to break the glass before you could press the firebell. This lent itself to all sorts of excitement and the boys leapt off the burning ship in a mass of moving bodies on the floor after having made all sorts of ringing noises.

Here again one sees all the quick change in the play from phantasy to reality when ideas from the real world are combined with make-believe; the boys, for example, pretended to eat food but they felt that the ship must run on petrol though they also seemed a little confused about the sort of oil used.

Mike appears to have been the leader though suggestions made by the others were accepted and used.

A great deal of learning is going on. Norman for example (observation 2) fetched a crane which he brought into his brick play. He experimented with raising and lowering the crane and was quite anxious when he thought he had broken it. An observer who was at hand watching the play was able to suggest what needed to be done and he was able to make things right for himself. Although he was playing alone one feels he had a secret longing to be included in some one else's play, as when he remarked somewhat pathetically that 'they', meaning the girls, could choose to put on dressing-up clothes and boys, he felt, couldn't. He returned to his bricks just a little sadly.

Alice (observation 8) sat happily alone building a little house around her, humming to herself and her doll. She was not so withdrawn in her own play, however, that she was not ready to accept a sweet when David offered her one.

Brick play is sometimes restricted for children because there are not enough bricks; they are too small and similar in size and shape and the space in which the play goes on is too restricted. Play out-of-door with large boxes, planks, etc., does give children the opportunity to make large structures which they can get inside or on top of. Unfortunately most of the things children build have to be taken to pieces and put away at the end of the day as there is no room to leave them. Young children, however, have often finished with an activity when they have made it and played in it for some time. They are ready to start again the next day, either with new ideas or the old ones adapted and changed to fit another occasion.

11
Water play

1

Margaret fills a washing-up liquid bottle from another plastic bottle, singing, 'We'll drink-a, drink-a to Lily the pink-a, pink-a.' Peter, holding a plastic container, shouts, 'Let's have a go,' and blows down a piece of rubber tubing into a bowl. Margaret empties the bottle, pouring it from above her head. It hits the water with a splash. She repeats this several times, chanting, 'It's raining, it's pouring.' Peter chants the same song. He then takes a funnel, puts it on his head, and says, 'I'm a monster.' They play a little longer and then wander off, taking their aprons off as they go.

2

Trudy plays with the water, gathering the water-play toys around her. She argues with Alison and grabs a plastic bottle and squeezes it under the water, watching the bubbles which appear as there is some soap powder in the water. She cups the foam and says, 'It's gorgeous,' blows into it and makes more bubbles, collects more in her hands and blows again. Alison picks up a teapot, fills and empties it six times, each time pouring from a greater height.

Trudy picks up a bowl and pretends it is a cup, Alison fills it with water and pretends she is making tea. 'Look!' she says, 'we're having a tea party,' and she scoops up some foam to make sugar. Both children play about a little longer and then go and dry their hands on their towels.

3

Tracy goes to the water-play, followed by Paulette, who picks up a plastic spoon and swishes it about in the water. She then picks up a plastic bottle shaped like a pig and says, 'Give the elephant a spoonful of medicine.' She empties the water out of the pig and says, holding it towards Tracy, 'Here, take it.'

Paulette pours some water into a spoon and then into the mouth of the pig. She puts her little finger into its mouth and pretends to take its temperature, saying, 'The elephant is ill, we must operate.' Tracy holds a funnel, as if it were some sort of instrument for testing the eyes, on a plastic bottle shaped like a tortoise. Paulette pours from two washing-up bottles she has filled with water, then fills one and pours it into the second, now empty, bottle saying, 'I'm making more medicine.' They continue pouring and talking for a few minutes longer.

4

Dilly is playing by herself with the water. She picks up the tubing and fits it to the funnel and, as the water runs out of the tubing, tries to catch it in a bowl. She then covers the bowl with a rubber glove, puts more water in a plastic bottle and pours that over the glove. She then says she is going to be a fireman and shouts, 'Do, do, dodo.' She holds the funnel with the tubing attached to it and as the water comes out she pretends it is a fireman's hose. Holding the hose with both hands she clutches one end to the lower part of her stomach and points the other end to the water trough, repeating this several times.

5

Susi goes to the water-play, collects all the water toys that are on the floor and puts them in the water. She takes the caps off the plastic bottles, fills them and squirts the contents. Dilly approaches and Susi shouts, 'Go away.' Dilly walks round the water-play trough and stands opposite Susi. Susi picks up a rubber doll and squashes her under the water, pulls her out by her feet, flings her down and shouts, 'I haven't had that yet,' pointing to a rubber glove. Dilly says, 'You've already had it.' Andrew comes along and joins in. He holds a funnel and inserts a hose-pipe. Dilly fits a hose-pipe into a bottle, fills it with water and pours

*it into Andrew's funnel. Andrew shouts, 'We can do it' as he
watches the water flow into the bottle. He asks Dilly for a cap,
but the one she produces is too big.*

*Richard joins the play, announcing that his mother is going
to buy him a train-set; no one appears to take any notice. Richard
and Dilly suddenly start saying, 'Der, der, der, der,' making hand
movements as if they were directing the traffic and driving a
car.*

*Andrew follows suit, saying that he is a baby one and making
hand movements as if he were driving a car too. Andrew and
Dilly call out, 'splish, splash, splish, splash,' pulling the tubing
between them as if it were a cracker.*

6

*Robin has a bowl of soapsuds and a pipe in front of him. He is
going to blow bubbles and is so charmed and excited about his
soapy bowl that he holds back, contemplating it with a quiet
rather mysterious smile as if no one knows its joys but he. Then
he buries his nose in the mixture and to his complete surprise he
suddenly sneezes as the soap powder goes up it. For a moment he
looks angry as if saying to himself, 'How dare you do that to
me!', then he laughs, picks up his pipe and starts to blow.*

7

*Michael and Russell are playing in the sink with the transparent
tubing fixed to two tins. Michael fills his tin from the tap but the
water runs away down the tube towards Russell. He lifts his tin
and the water runs back to Michael. They continue doing this
for some time. Michael then joins two tins with the transparent
plastic pipe, saying to a nearby adult, 'Here hold this blue one.'
He then watches the water run along into the blue tin from the
red one. He raises and lowers his tin to control the flow of water,
peering into each tin in turn. The adult points out the level of the
water which can be seen in the pipe and Michael makes it move
by raising and lowering the tin.*

*He then floats a small flat tin on the water, saying, 'It sinks,
it won't sink.' Then he puts a golf ball into the tin and says, 'It sinks,
now, it's forcing it.' He then puts in nails and other heavy things*

and again says, 'It's forcing it.' He puts a ping-pong ball on the surface of the water under the tap, turns on the tap and discovers that the ball jumps about. He goes on experimenting for a short time and then runs off to dry his hands.

8

Robert who is 3½ spends 25 minutes at water-play. Most of the time he fills a plastic bucket and then empties it. Then he turns on the tap, fills a plastic bottle, squeezes it until it is empty, then refills it, this time squeezing the water into the bucket and emptying the bucket when it is full into the sink. He does not talk at all but sings quietly to himself.

Children who come either to a Nursery School or to an Infant School, or who join an informal group of children, have generally learned a number of things about the way materials behave. They have compared things and seen their similarities and differences. They have observed and reacted to the weather, listened to thunder, watched water running out of taps and down plug-holes, seen that it collects in pools and drips off roofs.

They have asked numerous questions about the things they have seen, sometimes bringing magic to bear on the answers they have received. Their ability to use language has been an important factor in the understanding and development of logical thought.

In water-play the younger children appear to be continually experimenting with the feel of water. They watch it as it pours from the teapot's spout (observations 1 and 2). They listen as the water is squeezed out of bottles.

Snatches of the outside world impinge on their play. They are reminded of pop songs and often sing to themselves. Perhaps they are reminded too of the song from *Mary Poppins*, 'A spoonful of sugar makes the medicine go down,' as they give the elephant a spoonful of water (observation 3). There is a great deal of fun and enjoyment. Alison (observation 2) remarks quite spontaneously that, 'It's gorgeous.' Robert (observation 8) is quite overcome with delight as he blows his bubbles.

All sorts of phantasies appear; Trudy (observation 2) pretends she is making tea, turning the foam into sugar, while Peter with the greatest of ease becomes a monster by simply putting a funnel on his head (observation 1).

Paulette and Tracy (observation 3) are not only reminded of remembered songs but of illness. When Paulette feeds the pig with water from a spoon and suggests taking a temperature, she puts her finger in the pig's mouth.

Dilly, playing alone, is reminded (observation 4) of the fireman's hose and the fire brigade when she picks up a piece of tubing. Perhaps, too, when she is clutching it with both hands and holding it to her stomach and pointing the other end into the water trough she is unconsciously, in phantasy, linking it with some of her own anxieties and fears in relation to her own toilet training. These fears and anxieties must not be underrated; they are often remembered with misery long afterwards in adulthood.

The children move easily from one dramatic situation to another and Richard and Dilly (observation 4) are suddenly reminded of moving vehicles, when Richard announces quite out of the blue that his mother is going to buy him a train set. They both immediately start making traffic noises and driving imaginary cars.

Feelings of aggression appear. Susi shows these feelings towards Dilly when she comes to play, by shouting, 'Go away,' but she works out her hostility on the rubber doll which she squeezes angrily under the water. She shows verbal aggression when she accuses Dilly of not letting her have the rubber glove to play with (observation 5).

There is obvious delight in success and achievement when Andrew shouts (observation 5), 'We can do it.'

Children's amazing adaptability is always present and they use whatever comes to hand to serve the drama of the moment. They are constantly reminded of how one thing, because of its similarity, can be used to replace something else.

Learning how water behaves constantly appears as part of their water-play even if they sometimes make up magic reasons rather than logical ones for what they see happening.

Michael and Russell (observation 7) watched water finding its own level, saw things which floated and sank, asked questions, experimented and tried different ways of using their tins and plastic tubing. They tested things out to see what would happen and what was, and was not, successful.

Often (observation 8) a long time can be spent filling and emptying, squeezing and pouring, as if a child is trying fully to understand the behaviour of this exciting material called water.

12

Hospital play

1

Joy and Debra are dressed as nurses and a doll is tucked up in the hospital bed. Joy suggests Debbie be the mother saying, 'If you leave your little girl here, she might cry, she might scream.' Debbie insists she is the doctor. 'I'll make the dolly better, she vomits, doesn't she? I've got a medical tablet for her.' Joy says, 'Oh, dear, don't give her that tablet. Wait,' and she runs off. Debbie talks to herself: 'She's eat that tablet. Give her some more now.' She sits down on the chair close to the bed and strokes the doll's hair very gently and dreamily. Suddenly she gets up and runs off, but in a minute she returns with Stephen who is pretending to be ill. Debra sweeps the covers off the doll. Mark arrives and says he'll be the doctor and puts on a white coat. Stephen is now tucked up in bed. He says, 'Give me two dolls. I want two babies to have in bed. Can I have a tablet?' He says to Mark, 'It's not for you, it's for the man who's dead; can I have another one?' He examines the two dolls all over very carefully, exploring their bodies with his fingers. Joy has now returned. She has collected some very small sweets and she is carefully putting them into a bottle. 'Yes,' she says, 'you can have another tablet in a minute.'

Mark says in a very authoritative voice, 'You have to have two tablets a day and no more.' The patient meanwhile is becoming rather tired of waiting for the doctor. He plays around with the two dolls, examining them all over. He remembers where he is and plays dead.

Mark says, 'Show your belly please? Can I have the tablets now?' *He squeezes Stephen's stomach quite hard and Stephen pretends to be very ill indeed.*

Joy tries to bandage Stephen's stomach but finds it too difficult so puts it round his knee instead. Mark says he will have to stay in bed for ten days but he'll come and see him at 10 o'clock in the middle of the night. He is just going when he decides he will look at Stephen's stomach again. This time he pushes it with a plastic phial.

Joy says in a very worried voice, 'Do you think he'll die?' Stephen wails that he wants a drink of water.

Mark says to Debbie, who is trying to get some of the tablets out of the bottle, 'I'll give the tablets. It's a bit dangerous for you.' Mark then says firmly, 'Right, he can go home because someone else is dead.' Stephen gets up and changes place with Mark who now becomes the patient.

2

Sharon is in the home corner dressed as a nurse. She is busily looking after a doll in a pram. Four boys are looking at the hospital apparatus. Andrew has a stethoscope round his neck. The boys examine the bandages and cotton wool. Andrew says, 'We're all doctors.'

Christopher has a wad of cotton wool and keeps touching a doll's face and ears with it. He flinches as he does this as if he were hurting the doll.

Andrew and Christopher say again that they are both doctors and they argue together about this.

Sharon is trying to bandage Beverley's leg, but Beverley rejects this attention. Sharon says officiously, 'I think I'd better get you into the bed,' but Beverley still refuses, so Sharon gets her doll; she has given up trying to get Beverley to comply with her wishes.

Andrew now produces a bandage and puts it round Beverley's wrist and she passively accepts it.

Sharon announces that she is going to be dead now. She lies down on the bed, weakly calling, 'Doctor, doctor.' Christopher goes over, shakes some imaginary powder over her and leaves her. Sharon tries to get some attention by laughing, but without much success.

Andrew tells Sharon to get out of bed as she is to be the nurse.

Andrew powders the doctor's neck as he leans over Beverley bandaging her wrist. Christopher says firmly, 'You don't do that to doctors.'

Beverley is at last persuaded to get into bed. She is carefully tucked in by Andrew, who then leaves her to be looked after by Sharon. Beverley keeps 'crying' and Sharon becomes very solicitous, tucking her in, arranging her pillows, etc.

Andrew pounces on the stethoscope which has been dropped by Christopher and there is a tussle when Christopher discovers his loss.

Beverley complains that her hand still hurts and that the nurse has taken the bandage off. Christopher listens very carefully to her chest and then tells Sharon to look after her.

Beverley still continues to scream and Sharon says, 'What's wrong, are you dead? Are you better? Come on, you're coming for a walk with me.' They sit at the table in the home corner and then Sharon suddenly decides she will get Beverley back to bed again. She fails, however, and then decides to get back into bed herself. Christopher picks up the stethoscope and listens to a boy's arm. When Beverley takes the stethoscope herself and attempts to use it, Christopher says, 'Men have those, but not nurses.'

Beverley has now dressed herself as a nurse and she comes over to Sharon saying, 'Come on, you're having a typhoid injection.' She rubs Sharon's arm with cotton wool and then without warning pinches her arm so hard that Sharon begins to cry.

Beverley says she is sorry and Sharon gets out of bed saying she is going to paint. Both children wander off to the painting easels and pick up brushes.

3

Frances and Judy fuss over beds in the hospital corner with their dolls. Judy says, 'I'll get the baby ready' and she undresses the doll, saying that she has the measles. Frances attends to the bed and remarks that her baby has 'head trouble' and will have to keep her hat on. Judy powders her doll, re-dresses her and tucks her up in bed.

Alice passes, wheeling a doll in a pram, and says that her baby is ill too. Frances takes the doll carefully out of the pram and in a very business-like way starts to undress her. Judy says, 'I'll

examine her and you can examine the next baby that comes in.'
The stethoscope is used, the doll is powdered, and Frances says
to Alice, 'She's got poison so she'll be in hospital for six weeks.'

Alice moves nonchalantly away, leaving her baby, and plays
with some sand nearby. Her baby is offered back to her again but
she refuses to take her and says she's not playing any more.
Frances and Judy call after her somewhat mockingly, saying,
'Silly old bean-dress, silly old bean-dress.'

They continue to play when Judy suddenly asks, apparently
quite out of the blue though she is busy undressing her doll and
this may have suggested the question to her, 'What did your
Carol do, you said you'd tell me and you forgot.' (Carol is prob-
ably Frances's sister.) Frances hesitates and giggles and then
says, 'Oh she got up in the middle of the night, put on her best
knickers and did acrobats in the middle of the street.' Judy, not
to be outdone, says that she does that too, also in her best knickers
in the middle of the street in the night. They then return to
busily tucking up their dolls.

Janet goes by on a tricycle. They call out to her, suggesting
that she should come and play with them. Janet refuses and
Judy and Frances jump up, pull off their nurses' costumes and
run off to play somewhere else.

Hospital play by a group of young children is, of course, on the
surface all about what happens, or what they imagine happens,
when they go to hospital or are ill.

Much of it shows that the children do know something about
hospital procedure. Joy is aware (observation 1) that tablets
are often a part of being ill. Beverley knows about injections
(observation 2); she had actually had one quite recently and
when she pinched Sharon's arm, making her cry, she was pre-
sumably remembering, perhaps unconsciously, the unpleasant
prick and the sharp pain she herself had experienced during
the operation. The children, too, were familiar with stethoscopes
and bandages. Mark takes over the doctor's rôle (observation 1)
quite confidently and is sure that in his position it is he who
should give the tablets as they are part of the responsibility of the
doctor and they can be dangerous, therefore mere nurses are not
allowed to administer them. Joy, too, is a little concerned about

the danger involved in taking tablets when she says, 'Don't give her that tablet, wait.' On the other hand the patients often clamour for some. Powdering them seems a safer and easier way of dealing with the sick, and dolls and other children get a good deal of imaginary powder sprinkled over them.

Mark, as the doctor, speaks in an authoritative way as if he is completely in charge of the situation.

Stephen is interested in babies and where they come from, and feels that being in bed is something to do with the whole procedure. He insists that he had two in bed with him (observation 1). Whether he is mixed up between the rôle of mother and father it is difficult to decide; in any case he examines the two dolls very carefully, poking them everywhere with his fingers as if trying to discover what babies are like and where the mysterious creatures come from.

There seems some confusion in children's minds about being ill and being dead and it appears possible to be both at the same time.

The anxiety about death is one that concerns us all and is certainly part of children's thinking. If a loved parent dies it seems to them deprivation at its most devastating in the form of separation from those they love. Often they cannot grasp that the parent did not want to die and leave them. Children feel they could have lived if they had really wanted to and tried. This of course makes them miserable and guilty as they feel it must be their fault if mother or father didn't really want to stay with them enough to go on living.

The children in these observations showed that they tended to think that death was reversible (young children sometimes do); that you could die and become alive again all in a moment and this can be, perhaps, a comforting phantasy.

At the same time, children see and hear more about death and illness in hospital, on TV, than they used to, or rather, in the Victorian era, death at least tended to be linked with a happy and satisfying after-life in heaven—a hope which is often denied to children now, with our doubts about the hereafter. This perhaps brings the topic closer to children's conscious minds today, even if it has always been a part of their unconscious.

Groups of young children when hospital play is available are able to work through some of their deeper fears and anxieties about illness and dying.

As far as one could tell these children were not obsessed by dying, though Joy does say in a very worried voice, 'Do you think he'll die?' and when Beverley is screaming, Sharon says, 'What's wrong? Are you dead? Are you better?' and insists upon taking her for a walk as if to reassure them both that Beverley has recovered and there is no chance of her dying.

Both doctors and nurses get a feeling of power as they deal with the dolls or other children as patients. This in itself gives them a feeling that they can control illness, so children and dolls often recover quite quickly from the most serious of diseases.

Changes of rôle take place in a few seconds. You may be a seriously ill patient, a nurse, or a doctor but you need not stay in that position any longer than you want to. Mark (observation 1) decides he would rather be the patient for a change and Stephen gets up out of the bed for Mark to take his place.

There is always something exciting to children in suggesting bad behaviour, either a doll's or a sibling's, and on occasion to boast about their own naughtiness is attractive. For Frances to accuse Carol (probably her sister) of doing acrobats in her best knickers in the street at night sounds the most terrible of crimes but Judy, not to be outdone, says she has done it too. Both children were probably aware that this was just a phantasy on their part; nevertheless it gave them a nice feeling of indulgement in forbidden behaviour of the most alarming kind.

In spite of the occasional aggressive behaviour with either the dolls or other children, a good deal of kindly tucking up and smoothing of blankets goes on in connection with nursing and caring for the sick. Of course, if a bandage cannot be put round the victim's tummy the arm does equally well, and this doesn't trouble children at all.

The remembrance of past days

The Memories of childhood have no order, and no end

DYLAN THOMAS

How is play remembered by those who look back on their own childhood? How did they play? What do they recollect which seemed to have real significance for them? Have they been able to put it into a language which can be shared by others?

Some autobiographies contain glimpses of play which emerge as vivid and exciting because of the delight and the intensity of the experiences they evoked. These experiences may not have happened in exactly the way described, but the feeling is there clothed in language which takes the reader back in time to memories of his or her own childhood.

It is not the elaborate and complicated toys that seem to be the ones that children remember; rather is it the simpler ones which encouraged phantasy play of all kinds.

Some descriptions of play leave one with a feeling of happiness and serenity. Here was a child or here were children not only dearly loved but with understanding parents. Or here were children whose play was so intense and dramatic that it left a never-to-be-forgotten impression.

Often those who write children's books are able to bring to life imaginative and dramatic experiences which must have their roots in their own early lives. *Bevis*[1] (Richard Jefferies) describes the delights of a few weeks in the life of a boy when, in the Wiltshire countryside, he and his friend Mark had the most enthralling of times together: a phantasy life that was free, creative and as vivid as reality, with a background of wind and water, dew on the grass and singing birds.

Edith Nesbit remembers all the misdeeds it is possible for children to commit in their play and describes them in her children's books from the child's viewpoint. Kenneth Grahame in *The Golden Age*[2] emphasises the gulf that can exist between children and their elders; where the children see a place elf-haunted, a wood alive with pirates, a river whose source is the most exotic of marvels, their elders see nothing.

Here is phantasy play as described by Dylan Thomas when he and his friend Jack played at Indians together; it is easy to imagine and identify with this play among the grass and the bushes in the scramble and rush of two small boys lost and absorbed in their game :

Down the thick dingle Jack and I ran shouting, scalping the brambles with our thin stick hatchets, dancing, hallooing. We skidded to a stop and prowled on the bushy banks of the stream. Up above, sat one-eyed, dead-eyed, sinister, slim, ten-notched Gwilyn, loading his guns in Gallow's Farm. We crawled and rat-tattered through the bushes, hid, at a whistled signal, in the deep grass, and crouched there, waiting for the crack of a twig or the secret breaking of boughs.

On my haunches, eager and alone, casting an ebony shadow, with the Gorsehill jungle swarming, the violent, impossible birds, and fishes leaping, hidden under four-stemmed flowers the height of horses, in the early evening in a dingle near Carmarthen, my friend Jack Williams invisibly near me, I felt all my young body like an excited animal surrounding me, the torn knees bent, the bumping heart, the long heat and depth between the legs, the sweat prickling the hands, the tunnels down to the eardrums, the little balls of dirt between the toes, the eyes in the sockets, the tucked-up voice, the blood racing, the memory around and within flying, jumping, swimming, and waiting to pounce. There, playing Indians in the evening I was aware of myself in the exact middle of a living story, and my body was my adventure and my name. I sprang with excitement and scrambled up through the scratching brambles again.

Jack cried : 'I see you.' He scampered after me, 'Bang! Bang! you're dead.'

But I was young and loud and alive, though I lay down obediently.

'Now you try and kill me,' said Jack. 'Count a hundred.'[3]

Here is Vladimir Nabokov playing alone a wonderful and fantastic game, though he does not tell us its meaning, only the feeling of excitement and pleasurable fear as he crawled through a tunnel of darkness behind a couch pursued, perhaps, by a host of imagined terrors.

With the help of some grown-up person, who would use first both hands and then a powerful leg, the divan would be moved several inches away from the wall, so as to form a narrow passage which would be further helped to roof snugly with the divan's bolsters and close up at the ends with a couple of its cushions.

I then had the fanstastic pleasure of creeping through that pitch-dark tunnel, where I lingered a little to listen to the singing in my ears—that lonesome vibration so familiar to small boys in dusty hiding places—and then, in turn a burst of delicious panic, on rapidly thudding hands and knees, I would reach the tunnel's far end, push its cushion away, and be welcombed by a mesh of sunshine on the parapet under the canework of a Viennese chair.[4]

This play world of Vladimir Nabokov behind the divan, just an ordinary piece of furniture to the adult, became for him, a very small boy, a mysterious undertaking in time and space. Like a mouse, with a mouse's-eye view, he crawled down his long passage until at last he burst out into the sunshine. So one is reminded again of the largeness of the world to this pigmy-sized creature, the child.

Children can infuse drama into what could be the most domestic of pleasures, play with dolls; and what, one wonders, was behind the frightening and horrific play which Wilmett, the eldest sister of Mary and Phyllis Bottome exacted when she invented the game called 'Christian Martyrs'?

This was not a game I whole-heartedly liked, [Phyllis Bottome says] though it was desperately dramatic. It involved, and Wilmett made it a point of conscience that it should involve the giving up of a doll or two to be burnt alive—seldom her own dolls, which were, I must admit, in better repair than mine. It was not, however, really pleasant to me to think of even my oldest doll being burned alive. There were moments when I wondered if martyrdom was worth it. But I must confess there was something intensely exciting in the whole affair—a gladiatorial thrill, I suppose. All the dolls in the house were dragged out to sit in a circle and hear the chosen martyr make her Confession of Faith. She made it. Wilmett pronounced the sentence. Mary and I were allowed—nay, commanded—to turn down our thumbs; then the Executioner—also Wilmett, and I did not envy her this important rôle—placed the dedicated doll in the centre of the nursery fire, and we all sat back and watched it burn. I could just bear it, for sawdust—and in those days dolls were mostly made of sawdust—burns quickly; until one awful day when a kid doll was chosen as a martyr—and I think that not even Wilmett knew that kid dolls writhe.[5]

Wilmett appears in the autobiography, not only as the leader of the three children but as in some instances a demanding bully, expecting her sisters to obey her. She made up and took part in all their games, seeing to it that she played the central rôle. She enjoyed and wanted power.

When she inaugurated the game of burning the dolls was she projecting her angry feelings on to them and then punishing them by burning them to assuage her own guilt? Was she jealous of her two sisters and did she punish them by burning their dolls in a dramatic way in which she was mistress of the situation? Wilmett had had to carry, as a child, more than her fair share of responsibility and perhaps there was a good deal of unresolved hostility towards the two sisters who took up so much of her time and energy, so she must needs gets her own back in her play.

Pearl Buck in her autobiography conveys the feeling of utter contentment which can result from really satisfying play when she describes her private world under the veranda of her home in China.

> My early memories are not of parents, however, but of places. Thus our big, whitewashed, brick bungalow, encircled by deep, arched verandas for coolness, was honeycombed with places that I loved. Under the verandas the beaten earth was cool and dry, and I had my haunts there. The gardener made a stove for me from a large Standard Oil tin with one side cut away. He lined the three sides with mud mixed with lime and then set into it a coarse iron grating. When I lit a fire beneath this and put in charcoal I could really cook, and of course I cooked the easy Chinese dishes I liked best and that my amah taught me. I had a few dolls but my 'children' were the small folk of the servants' quarters or the neighbours', and we had wonderful hours of play, unsupervised by adults, all of whom were fortunately too busy to pay us heed. I remember going to bed at night replete with solid satisfaction because the day had been so packed with pleasurable play.[6]

Alison Uttley's play (though the actual story where she describes it is about a child growing up in the country) is obviously drawn from her own childhood and shows how her play impinged on the tasks of the adult world where Susan is able to stir the milk. Her pleasure in playing at being grown-up is satisfied by doing this, for she is not only imitating the grownups, but she has almost become one for a brief moment. This can be real play to a child particularly when there is no insistence that she continues. In fact, Susan is called away when she would have liked to go on.

> Susan played outside in the dusk, running races with herself, skipping up and down the cobbled farm-yard, tossing a ball in the air to hit the sycamore tree, singing and talking to Roger, who ran up and down, nearly wild to get loose. Then she met the farm men walking slowly home with cans of milk, steadying them with both hands as they swayed on the yokes across their shoulders. She collected the eggs from the window ledge in the barn where Becky had left them and carried them to the dairy in a large flat basket. The men put the milk-cans in the

stone troughs at the back door to cool whilst they harnessed the horse.

'Susan, Susan, come and stir the milk,' called Tom Garland, and Susan ran out and seized a hazel wand which lay clean and bright, across the trough. She dipped it in the frothy, foamy pails and swirled the milk round and round, sending little splashes of cream over into the water, watching them fall like funnels of opal deep down till they became one with the water. The stars came out and twinkled in the great clean-water trough, and she dipped her wand in to break them into fragments.

'Come on, that's enough. You're spilling the milk and messing the drinking water. Get away, you're no use,' and her father pushed her aside to take the milk to be measured.[7]

For children to take part spontaneously in doing what grown-up people do is play whose pleasures are perhaps under-rated. They always love their child-sized objects, which are similar to those their parents use but to struggle with man-sized tools also has a charm all its own.

Freya Stark, in remembering her childhood's play, says that in her memories it is the feeling connected with the activities which is so clear to her.

As clear as at the age when it happened, more so because more intelligible.

One is of my doll's house my father built out of old boxes, swinging open with all its doors and windows and muslin curtains attached, and closing again on the dolls within, which seemed alive but less comprehensible than people or animals. They were not things to play with like a cat or a dog, but malevolent : I disliked them and poured tea into the mouth of one with a secret pleasure over the ruin of its sawdust stuffing, not diminished by the fact that it was Vera's doll.[8]

Perhaps as one would expect of Freya Stark, it was the real world of living and growing things that she found so enchanting and full of magic to play with.

We lived in the garden [she wrote in describing one of her homes] in that world which vanishes—though I can still think of it as the real world now and then—where there is no barrier between human and no human existence, and even the inanimate object has its independent life, a target for passion. . . . The garden gave that delight of something going on all the time, which the world gives later to happy people. It was the world with a vagueness of chaos and the unknown beyond its neat wooden palisades.[9]

Children think of all sorts of things to play with when they are bored and if none of their own toys is available they find something. They may, of course, get punished as a result but sometimes the punishment is worth the fun of the play; or so Gwen Raverat felt.

I was only once spanked that I can remember. I had been put to rest after lunch on my mother's bed, under the muslin curtains, which fell down from the hanging canopy. Now resting is a foolish theory, from which many parents suffer. It is far too exhausting for children, it is really only suitable for the old. I used to get absolutely worn out inventing games to play during the ages when I was condemned to 'rest'; so that by the time the rest was over, I really did need a rest. However, this time I enjoyed myself. I found on the dressing-table a stick of red lip-salve. The white wall-paper was nearly framed by the bed-curtains; so I began a fine, bold wall-painting, in enormous swoops and circles. It was like frescoing the walls of Heaven. But I was interrupted, and my father was told to spank me with a slipper. It didn't hurt and I did not mind a bit. But I never forgot the joy of wall-painting.[10]

Here are memories from perhaps a more leisurely period, at least for children from pleasant and comfortable homes.

Enchanted memories of the drawing-room after tea remain. Among the toys brought out for us to play with on the floor was one that delighted me so much that even now if I pass a market-place on a sunny day I can almost feel the soft comfort of the carpet under me as I gazed at the little gaily-painted greengrocer's stall that my grandmother set before me. Tiny glossy oranges could be picked up between finger and thumb and rolled into a miniature barrel. Minute bunches of carrots and crates of cauliflowers could be moved about the stall without ever detracting from its charm. The big wooden letters, hewn by the estate carpenter, were interesting too but in a different way. My grandmother would arrange them on the floor in biblical texts which we learnt to recognize in their entirety long before we could read. GOD IS LOVE; KNOCK AND IT SHALL BE OPENED UNTO YOU; SEEK AND YE SHALL FIND were all as familiar patterns as the Noah's Arks and Gardens of Eden she built for us with the wooden bricks, wedges and blocks from the timber yards, polished by two centuries of handling and each one known individually by every grandchild.[11]

It is sad to think that some of the orphanages, foster-homes, and sanatoriums to which young children were sent during the early part of this century, not really so very long ago, had a very different method of dealing with children and their toys. Even today we do not always realize that certain toys or objects may mean something very special to a child : a link between themselves and home, almost an extension of themselves. They may not know what this object or toy really stands for, they know only that it is dearly loved and precious and that they must hold on to it like an anchor.

Janet Hitchman describes what happened to one of her dearly-loved possessions.

I had taken with me to the sanatorium a little teddy-bear about six inches long. It had for many years been a kind of fetish, going everywhere with me. It was small enough to go into a pocket, but now I had no pockets it spent most of its time tucked into the top of my bloomers. It was now rather flabby and the sawdust was leaking through a hole in one of the seams. I took it to the sewing-room to see if Miss Taylor would put some more stuffing in and stitch it up. Nurse Jones was there.

'What do you want !' she barked at me.

Ignoring her I said, 'Please Miss Taylor, can you mend my Teddy?'

'Miss Taylor hasn't any time for that rubbish,' cut in Nurse Jones before the seamstress could answer, and snatching the bear from me she flung it on the fire. 'Get out,' she ordered. Hardly able to take in what had happened I went, and as I closed the door I heard Miss Taylor say, 'That wasn't necessary,' and Nurse Jones' reply, 'I can't bear that kid. It was a filthy thing anyway; full of germs.' Now I made no attempt to understand or placate this woman—the war was on. . . . I think I made life as miserable for her as she did for me.[12]

Janet Hitchman was old enough and determined enough to get her own back; many children, however, are too small and helpless to do anything but weep in sorrow and despair.

Reading what others have written, and how they have felt and reacted, often stimulates our own imaginations and we, too, suddenly remember experiences from the past whose very existence we had forgotten. This in its turn can help us to understand and to feel with the children we have under our care.

PART THREE

Where children play

Where the pools are bright and deep
Where the grey trout lies asleep,
Up the river and o'er the lea,
That's the way for Billy and me.

JAMES HOGG, *A Boy's Song*

14

Observations

Looking out over any large city nowadays from a railway carriage, from the street, from a top window, great blocks of flats seem to dominate the landscape, rising like huge giants dwarfing the small houses and shops that still remain, casting deep shadows on the ground.

In these large blocks live families with their children looking down from high windows onto pools of emptiness. With the street often so far below everything looks small; toy cars, toy people ceasing to have any reality to those watching them.

In blocks of this kind children have somehow to try and find places to play, to move, to explore, to discover adventure and to create their own gay, spontaneous world.

Dangers seem to lurk everywhere for those living in such blocks causing constant anxieties to parents.

Sometimes there are unprotected landings and balconies from which children can fall or throw their belongings, or unsupervised lifts which are so often used for unauthorized play that they easily go wrong; children may get trapped in them and everyone who has to struggle up long, unending flights of stairs with shopping, prams and babies is angry, upset and exhausted. Few blocks of flats are sound proof and this means that children's lively high spirits and natural movements must be drastically curtailed.

Large blocks of flats are lonely places with their maze of landings, passages, stairways and doors; families tend to shut themselves in their own small enclosures. The children, instead of widening their parents' contacts, helping them to make friends, are often a cause of friction and anxiety because they are mischievous, curious and noisy, and disturb and irritate everyone in their efforts to find amusement.

Flat dwellers tend to ask to be transferred to other accommodation as soon as they discover all the disadvantages they must put up with; thus the population is a shifting one and friends are difficult to make and keep.

If the older children can play round the blocks unsupervised, even though the environment is often very limited, young children need their mothers or some understanding and familiar adult near at hand. From a flat two or three storeys up a mother may sometimes be able to watch her child at play, but she can never reach him in a moment of crisis or danger and nor can the child reach her.

Without even considering the play-needs of children over eight living in large blocks of flats, and theirs are pressing enough, what of the younger ones?

We know that children are curious, lively, vigorous creatures influenced by the kind of environment in which they find themselves, learning all the time. They need above all things space to move and play freely in a rich and varied setting and the companionship of other children, and these needs are extremely difficult to satisfy in large blocks of flats. Children often merely view the world through vast expanses of plate glass, moving quietly around in rooms where every sound carries.

Obviously, when such blocks are built, areas for children, places where the elderly can sit in peace, facilities for boys and girls over eight and teenagers should be considered from the very beginning in the overall planning of the site; it is wasteful to add in a casual and haphazard way facilities that should have been thought of before the first bricks were laid.

Young children, for example, need a safe, attractive place where they cannot wander off into traffic-filled streets, annoy the ground-floor tenants by their shouts and laughter, and with toilet facilities near at hand.

They need opportunities for really active play, and equipment such as slides, swings and climbing apparatus of all kinds to challenge their skill and ingenuity, and in fact, a wealth of ingenious and imaginative material *is* available if only it can be set up.

Children want growing things around them—grass, trees, bushes, flowers which bring them into contact with the natural world; places where they can dig, mess with water and sand, use bricks, play with dolls; a spot to sit quietly sheltered from sudden rain storms or glaring sunshine. Paths are needed where tricycles can be ridden and dolls' prams pushed.

A feeling of safety and intimacy matters to young children, a setting where there is an adult to turn to for comfort and help. It isn't easy for a busy mother to be always there even if a pleasant place is provided where she can sit and watch her children.

The question of the supervision of the play area for young children in blocks of flats is indeed an urgent one.

If flat dwellers have their problems so do those who live in small houses on traffic-filled streets. Playing on the pavement or in the road is full of dangers and small children under eight are impulsive and quick moving and cannot be relied upon to remember the Highway Code.

It is true that the busy streets with shops, lights, noise and colour have more to offer children than the bleak areas often surrounding blocks of flats. They can play their traditional games outside their own front doors, meet their friends and discover a feeling of community in the narrow, congested streets. If the older children, however, can wander off farther afield and take a bus to a park or play centre, the under-fives certainly cannot and need to be constantly watched while they are playing. New housing estates can also be dreary places without the life, vitality and companionship of the city. Families can feel cut off from the life they knew, separated from relations and friends. Children can wander away when front gardens are unfenced, play around parked cars and lose themselves in the maze of small roads and often silent front lawns.

Perhaps the most fortunate parents are those with their own safe gardens, with money enough to provide the sort of play materials their children need. The professional parent sometimes finds it easier to make contacts, entertains more and so gets to know her neighbours more easily.

Such parents, of course, are often very aware of their children's need for companionship and an even more stimulating environment than they can provide. They too want a place for their children to play safely beyond the confines of home.

There is no question that the good Nursery School would be of untold value to all these families and their children.

In the city there are not nearly enough parks or adventure play-grounds where children can have exciting play, involving digging, building, climbing, making gang huts, lighting fires. London has about 2,000[1] waste sites which often lie unused for years, and no doubt other large cities have them too.

Adventure play-grounds are not really suitable for young children even when there is a leader in charge. They need some small corner fenced off with indoor accommodation as well as outdoor playing space.

If young children are going to be taken to parks for play there must be facilities for their mothers too; most children under eight are not allowed to travel any distance by themselves to play.

As the population grows, more flats and houses are built and roads become even more congested. No places will be left for children to play unless their needs are given first priority.

15

Provision for pre-school children

This year,
Next year,
Sometime,
Never.

Old Rhyme

The educational provision for children under five has always been inadequate and extremely slow and precarious in its development. We are deeply indebted to the early pioneers who saw the effects of poverty, overcrowding and malnutrition on the physical and mental health of young children and the need to do something positive about it.

Certain names inevitably spring to mind in this connection; Robert Owen in 1816 opened the first school at New Lanark, in Scotland, for children from the age of two years whose mothers were working in the mills; Sir William Mather in 1872, Miss Adelaide Wragge in 1900 and Miss Julia Lloyd in 1904 all founded what were then known as kindergartens, in Salford, Woolwich and Birmingham, for children living in the slums.

The name, of course, that is most closely associated with the general care of young children is that of Margaret McMillan, who worked tirelessly to better their conditions and who, with her sister Rachel, opened the first open-air Nursery School in Deptford in 1911 with six children.

The urgent need for more Nursery Schools was kept continually before the public eye by many other enthusiastic and hardworking men and women, but in spite of their efforts and the formation of The Nursery School Association in 1923 progress lagged far behind need. Whenever a financial crisis threatened, the money available for nursery education was either drastically cut or withdrawn altogether.

During the 1939–45 war a tremendous number of nurseries under the auspices of the then Ministry of Health were opened to care for the children whose mothers were needed in industry. When the war ended, however, many of them were closed.

The 1944 Education Act, which laid a duty on Local Authorities to provide Nursery Schools, Classes, or Wings was never implemented. Nursery Schools and Classes today have extremely long waiting lists and although many of them have become part-time, taking one group of children in the morning, and another in the afternoon, so doubling the number of children who can be catered for, the places available are totally inadequate.

Yet we are more aware than ever before of the importance of the early years and what the good Nursery School or Class can offer a child. It is not only the children from over-crowded homes who are in need, the more privileged children too, want and crave the facilities that nursery education can give them. What is the picture like at the moment?

Many of us hoped that in 1963 when the Central Advisory Council for Education (England) was asked by Sir Edward Boyle, the then Minister of Education, to consider the whole subject of Primary Education and the transition to secondary education that the subsequent report which would be published, would in its recommendations stress not only the need for more nursery provision, but would also underline the quality of the care which should be provided for young children.

This report published in 1966 and known as The Plowden Report[2] has proved disappointing as far as nursery provision is concerned.

It is often necessary to suggest some form of interim policy when shortages of staff and premises obviously make the ideal impossible to attain and this is acceptable for the time being. One feels, however, that the Plowden Report has laid down a permanent policy and a pattern for all forms of future Nursery school education that many feel was quite unsuitable.

It envisages the incorporation of many less well-trained adults in the Nursery School system. It says, in effect, that the day-to-day running of the nurseries should be in the hands of trained nursery assistants, though every 60 full-time places should be supervised by a qualified teacher. Thus a qualified teacher would be in charge of a nursery centre consisting of three groups of 20 children. If in single groups of 20 spread over a larger area, the qualified teacher would divide her time as she saw fit between them all. Each group of children would be in the charge of an experienced nursery assistant.

In the main these nursery assistants will be drawn from girls who have taken their Nursery Nurses Certificate (the N.N.E.B.). They will have attended Colleges of Further Education for a two-year course, but three-fifths of their time will be spent as helpers in Nursery Schools, Classes, Day Nurseries, etc. The training they receive and the examinations they take involve reading, study, observation and lectures, and sometimes after having completed their course they go on to a College to train for the teaching profession. On the whole, however, they are girls who leave school early and whom the Colleges of Education would find unsuitable from the academic point of view.

The N.N.E.B. training is extremely valuable as a pre-nursing, pre-marriage or in certain cases a pre-teaching course, but it is not sufficient in itself for the recipient to be given, with the help of another individual with the same training, the sole care of 20 children who attend in the morning and another 20 who come in the afternoon, 40 children in all, or 20 if they attend all day.

Looked at honestly, this policy implies that boys and girls under five are thought to need less intellectual ability on the part of those in charge than any other age group. Nursery Schools and Classes have always had a very close relationship with the parents and such contacts need skill and understanding on the part of the adult concerned—not an easy task to demand of a N.N.E.B. nursery assistant.

The life of the trained teacher would in such circumstances often be a very lonely one, with no one of her own background and training to consult with, while if she is away through illness 40 or perhaps 60 children will be without a fully trained member of staff available.

'There is a great threat here to the quality of the education of younger children which may set back the great advances in the application of knowledge during the last half century.'[2] Nowadays Nursery Schools and Classes often receive certain children who are disturbed or have some physical or mental handicap; such children need special skill and care if the wellbeing of the group as a whole is not to be jeopardized; their parents also may need very careful and sympathetic handling.

In relation to staffing, Dr. Wall, in his book, *Child of Our Time,* in suggesting that the community must make greater provision for the free play of children under seven or eight, also points out that the organized provision for the play of young children is not by itself sufficient.

He stresses not only the importance of the richness of the environment itself but the interaction of the children with the adults in charge—the stimulation at the right moment of activities, the talk by which experiences are enlarged and ideas fostered, and the way a background and setting can be planned to provide really vital and challenging opportunities. He goes on to make some extremely valuable and worthwhile points :

Even more important, however, than intellectual acquisitions, is the effect of an environment on the child's personal growth. Experience with other children and with adults other than the parents will in itself do much to supplement the efforts of the parents at socialization. But there is more than this. Socialization implies, of course, a reasonable standard of behaviour to others, experiences of giving and receiving, of cooperation, of antagonism and of anger as well as of affection and love; its acquisition is a slow process in which children have many back-slidings and in which they learn, through the experience of group or adult reactions against such things as ill-temper or aggression, painfully to control their impulses. We have, however, to ask ourselves whether this alone will suffice and whether some more direct effort should not be made.

Many adults grow up with perfectly adequate techniques of social integration—they are pleasant, relatively unaggressive, friendly—all that one might wish. They lack, however, insight into their own motives and prejudices and into those of others.

It is not suggested that one should teach young children the psychology of human motivation. However, adults and other children do make remarks and do impute motives. What is suggested, therefore, is that children should be helped to verbalize and to understand their own behaviour and that of others in an informal way. This, of course, demands of the adults concerned a considerably higher level of insight into themselves as persons, and a considerably greater knowledge of children than is usually possessed even by trained nursery or other teachers; and it implies that both training and selection of those who are to undertake this important task should be carefully considered.[3]

This statement provides food for a great deal of thought, particularly in relation to the staffing recommendations of the Plowden Report.

Some groups of children always seem to be particularly badly off as far as trained staff are concerned. Those boys and girls attending Day Nurseries (now under the umbrella of the Social Services Act) because their mothers are obliged to go out to work, have rarely had the luxury of a trained teacher in charge of their daily educational needs.

The Residential Nurseries (responsible to the Home Office) also tend to be staffed by young and constantly changing Nursery Nurses in the day-to-day care of the children. Looking after these children, who are deprived of a normal home life, desperately in need of love, stability and a rich and absorbing play-life, one begins to question the quality of the environment provided. The work is exhausting and demanding and those who undertake it give generously of their time and energy.

Knowing what we do of the vital significance of the early years and the needs of young children, how do we expect them to develop under the sort of changing conditions we would certainly not choose for our own children?

Perhaps it is time to reconsider the whole question of the personal and the general environment that is provided in the welfare state for these children today.

Recently, the play group movement is one that has made a phenomenal growth. It is impossible to say the actual number existing, but the Association has some 4,000 member groups in which probably 116,000 children are involved.

This is a voluntary movement which caters for small groups of children gathered together for play and using whatever accommodation can be found. The groups are largely staffed by parents, mothers helping and taking charge and sometimes receiving a small salary. As a rule these mothers have had no training, except perhaps attending a short course of lectures. Because the provision of Nursery Schools and Classes as part of our Educational system has been so pathetically slow (in January 1967 about 3.1 per cent of two- to four-year-olds were in Nursery Schools or Classes, and Local Authorities were officially restricted from expanding), Play Groups feel that they have done and are doing a very valuable job. They would now like to achieve official recognition and some form of training with a certificate awarded in any future Education Act.

On the whole, the Play Group movement is a middle-class one and fees are charged for attendance in order that the groups can buy equipment, pay the rent and someone to look after the children. Some Local Authorities, perhaps because they find it cheaper than opening Nursery Schools or Classes, give a grant for materials, perhaps pay a local adviser, or the fees for children whose parents could not otherwise afford to send them.

If disturbed, handicapped or neglected children are paid for and attend the Play Groups they can be difficult for the untrained staff to manage and the other mothers, quite naturally, tend to resent the time and energy these children demand.

The 'Save the Children Fund' has for some time organized Play Groups in the most needed areas but on rather different lines. They have roughly 96 groups and 16 in hospitals. They use trained Nursery Nurses and only in very exceptional circumstances rely on mothers helping. They have supervisors to advise and allow about £2,000 a year for each group, a sum sometimes paid by the Local Authority.

No one would deny that Play Groups have made a very valuable contribution to pre-school education. They have helped a very large number of children and parents and have influenced education as a whole. One must, however, be aware of their limitations.

Are we merely providing a second best for the pre-school child and tempting Local Authorities to take advantage of a cheap form of care?

In the poorer areas it will be much more difficult to staff the groups and find accommodation, and there will be less money available from the parents. Thus, there may easily develop one type of Play Group for the 'haves' and another for the 'have nots', thus dividing people who should be brought together.

Children, lucky enough to attend a Local Authority Nursery School or Class, would be in charge of a trained teacher receiving a teacher's salary. Play Group personnel would feel themselves to be second-class workers with a small remuneration for the work they were doing.

We would, in effect, be saying that children under five do not need expert guidance and education, and that an extremely inadequate training and qualification and all that that implies is good enough for them.

It is always a little precarious to rely on the enthusiasm of amateurs. Voluntary and poorly-paid help fluctuates as other interests arise and new ones become fashionable. Nor is the enthusiastic person, anxious to help, necessarily the most suitable.

Are draughty, uncomfortable halls and huts, often grubby and unattractive whatever improving efforts are made, often with no outdoor playing space, really good enough for our children? Perhaps for a couple of hours a day for the child from a comfortable and pleasant home, once or twice a week such conditions do not matter so much, but what of the child from the poor, overcrowded home with no play facilities?

Without in any way detracting from the good work the Play Groups have done we surely must think of them as an interim measure until more Nursery Schools and Classes are in existence. Any help the trained and experienced teacher can give to such groups during this period, when they are providing young children with play experiences they would otherwise be denied should be given. At the same time, we must be on the alert and not be prepared to accept anything but the best for pre-school children.

16

Play in the home

Mid pleasures and palaces though we may roam,
Be it ever so humble, there's no place like home.

JOHN HOWARD PAYNE, *Clari the Maid of Milan.*

Whatever the play facilities which the community may eventually
have to provide for the great majority of young children in
present-day society—particularly when we consider the conditions
under which many of them live— it must not be forgotten that a
child's home, however inadequate it may be, is all-important to
him and will be the first place in which he enjoys free and spontaneous play.

Almost from the moment of birth the well-loved baby is played
with. Many of the ordinary everyday experiences of living—being
dressed, bathed and fed, put to bed or taken out—are moments
when a loving mother turns the whole procedure into a game : a
game which includes a great deal of active love, of talk, naming
objects, finger plays and so on, and even if the baby is too small
to understand he keenly appreciates all the attention he is getting.
His mother, too, probably enjoys the play as much as he does and
is as thrilled with his responses as he is with her approval. At
Christmas he will be given presents, will even perhaps have a
Christmas tree, and though he may be too young to grasp what
it is all about, his parents feel they would like to celebrate and
remember even if the baby doesn't.

He will have his rattle, his teething ring, his cuddly toys, his
mobiles to watch as he lies in his cot or pram. Then he will have

his toys in his playpen or he will be around his mother's feet as she moves about the kitchen. He likes saucepans and spoons to play with, but he needs continual watching as he wriggles and crawls like an eel or staggers into, under, on, off and round everything within reach.

As he gets older he follows his mother about the house when she is sweeping and dusting, helping and hindering as best he can. In the evening he is delighted to find a new playmate in his father, who comes fresh to the fray when his mother's energy and ardour is flagging.

Young children need this constant interaction between themselves and their parents and siblings to be enjoyed and accepted and all the time they are absorbing a tremendous amount of knowledge about the world around them and the people in it and gaining experiences of all kinds. The first new human contacts they make are often friends and relations of the family who come along as interested and affectionate persons.

Some young children at an early age acquire a very special object, perhaps a bit of old towel, blanket or shawl, or a grubby teddy bear, to which they cling. It seems to comfort them in moments of stress, envelopes them in an aura of safety. It is something to hold on to, a bit of their world which they have somehow endowed with very special qualities. This 'transitional object' (as Dr. Winnicott calls it) may go everywhere with them, to strange houses, hospital, Nursery School, a link with all they love and hold precious and from which they cannot bear to be parted.

We may not understand why children have this need or why a particular object is so cherished, but it matters very much to them and it should be respected. Adults, too, have their symbols—a lucky charm perhaps given them by a mother or sweetheart, and which they carry with them everywhere.

Playthings for young children need not be expensive or elaborate and the ordinary kitchen often provides much that they enjoy.

So often older children are given costly objects which are very limited in the way in which they can be played with and are easily broken, for example, models of guns or weapons which fire bombs or missiles.

Toys such as these, even for imaginative play, which are wholly destructive, and whose only object really is to kill and destroy, seem to me not only unnecessary but harmful. They glamorize war, casting a superficial aura of amusement over what in reality is deadly and tragic, and only encourage children to take violence and destruction for granted.

No one minds little boys running around with toy pistols or bits of wood for guns, wearing belts and hats, shooting each other dead. They are getting rid of a lot of aggressive energy and doing no one any harm.

The toys we buy boys and girls should provide scope for all sorts of constructive, imaginative and creative play, should be able to sustain interest and be durable, while suggesting a variety of activities and not just dictating certain usages.

As children get older they may need less active help in their play from their parents as they are seeking companions of their own age; family involvement, however, is still very important. Children need to be read to, even when they can read for themselves. They want and enjoy family outings and picnics, to be taken to films, theatres and concerts. They want the active interest of their parents in their hobbies, collections, and creative achievements, not of course by constant criticism, interference or the demanding of standards a child cannot reach.

Some children revel in after-tea and after-supper play during the week and at weekends at home, perhaps dressing up and making up plays for their parents to see or playing happily with familiar and well-loved toys. Others love family games such as snakes and ladders, ludo, monopoly, scrabble or chess. Occasionally a boy or girl *has* to win in a game; it is really a pressing, urgent need as far as he or she is concerned and in the family circle this can be arranged. A blind eye can be turned on the child who sometimes cheats because he cannot bear always to lose.

This may sound as if one is just being weak and giving in to a child's selfish whim. This is not really so. Children are learning how to accept failure, but they can accept it more easily if they have had some successes on which to build. Some boys and girls fail too often and need their confidence in themselves reinforced in a variety of different ways.

It would be difficult to find a child even from a loving and secure home who hasn't at some time or other needed to cheat or steal, knowing quite well that this sort of behaviour is not socially acceptable. He has not, however, grown up to be a criminal or a jail bird.

Children do work these stresses and problems out for themselves in their day-to-day play, particularly when they learn from parental example and where the standards of behaviour expected of them are geared to their development.

Possessions are, on the whole, important to most of us. Children need to own things and have places to keep them safely.

Most of us as we learn to take care of and cherish our own belongings, begin to take care of other peoples' things, too. Children may need help over this, not by rigid rules and punishment, but by sensible standards and example.

So often it is the unloved and unwanted child who is pointlessly destructive. The rejected child, whether at home or in a residential establishment, who has never been satisfied with love seeks other substitutes to satisfy his needs. He steals food, praise and possessions and is envious and greedy for everything—but dissatisfied when he gets it—in order to try and fill the empty places within himself where love should have been.

All children are, of course, untidy from the adult's point of view. Their play is messy and unorganized. Their treasures are trivial, their demands excessive, their imaginative play difficult to understand. Yet, if we only have time to watch we learn so much about the children and, incidentally, a good deal about ourselves as these 'small editions' play out their lives before us.

Children want to share in grownup pursuits in a play way. Boys want to help their fathers and so feel manly and adult, or help their mothers, so identifying themselves with and taking the place of the man in the family. Girls want to act similarly, 'standing in' for mother and doing the things she does. This, of course, must be play and children must be able to opt out of their imaginary responsibilities.

The value of play at home and parental relationships should never be underestimated. Some children may be more fortunate than others, but every parent has a great deal to offer and the fun, appreciation and delight they get from their children is worth all the trouble and anxiety they sometimes cause.

It is always very easy just to make suggestions about children's play needs, particularly, perhaps, for those children who are round their mother's feet all day when there is limited space available for them to use; forgetting that many of the things that parents with a small garden or yard can do are often impossible for those living in large blocks of flats with small rooms.

What can one do under such circumstances?

A large ground sheet or piece of plastic spread on the floor for a small child to sit on when playing with a bowl of silver sand or water with objects to empty and fill, saves a mess all over the floor.

Most children, unless they have only got their pants on and nothing else, need something such as a rubber pinafore to keep them from soaking themselves. Some children can stand on a chair at the sink and play with water and if all this seems impossible bath time at night should be made into a really pleasant time for play with lots of things in the bath to have fun with.

Clay is an excellent material for children to use, but in the small home it is difficult to manage. Dough, however, is a very good substitute and it can be coloured with vegetable dyes if necessary. Young children can mould, pull and bang it (it doesn't matter if they put it in their mouths); the older child may want to make a ginger bread man or a bun and have it cooked in the oven.

The saucepans and wooden spoons that mother uses in the kitchen have already been mentioned as objects for play. Children will polish spoons, scrub potatoes or carrots, shell peas, sweep the floor with a little dust-pan and brush, play with empty boxes, screw top jars and cartons of all kinds. A big cardboard box full of harmless oddments keeps children happy for quite a while. Clothes pegs are very useful and a piece of line stretched between two chairs can be used to put pegs on by an energetic two-year-old.

Newspapers can be torn up (sitting on the ground sheet!), old magazines, boxes of Christmas cards or postcards can be looked at and talked about.

Dolls and cuddly toys need bits of material to wrap them in and boxes to put them to bed in. Rubber dolls can be bathed, soaped and dried endlessly, while dolls' clothes can be washed, and children love helping mother clean something.

Things to sort and match, corks, buttons (not very small things if children are still putting them in their mouths), etc., are enjoyed. Simple puzzles, fitting toys, pyramid rings, building beakers, hammer pegs, interlocking cubes, posting boxes, big wooden beads to thread (square ones roll less easily than round ones), small boxes of bricks, little cars and trucks of all kinds, are things that can be played with in small rooms. Newspaper and brown paper can be used with chalks, crayons and paints; chairs and clothes horses make lovely tents with old blankets and rugs.

All children need to learn something about the community in which they live, visit the post office, the shops, carry the wrapped loaf, be lifted up to post a letter, lick on a stamp, hand out the money in the bus or shop.

In the park they can be encouraged to use whatever equipment is available. A visit to a railway station, pet shop, market, etc. give children opportunities for all sorts of talk, question and imaginative play.

In the country they can collect pebbles, fir cones, feathers, moss, sticks, pick daisies and dandelions; little gardens can be made with moss and flowers in bowls and old cake tins, seeds, carrot tops can be planted; flowers arranged in little vases, collections of findings kept in little boxes and all these things can be done even with limited space.

The slightly older child loves making things from any waste material there is at hand and even though the results may look somewhat peculiar, to the child it is all wonderful. A large box into which one can put empty match boxes, cotton reels, scraps of paper and materials, spent matches, etc. will be useful on a wet afternoon.

As children will often eat burnt potatoes and sausages they have cooked themselves, so with younger children, and new foods and drink imbibed from dolls' plates and cups will often be accepted with relish when otherwise they would be indignantly refused.

Most children like dressing up in mother's old clothes, helping (though it may be hindering) father when he puts up a shelf, cleans the car, or goes out to post his football pools.

If pegs for clothes are put within a child's reach he can hang up his own coat, and get his slippers out of a slipper bag. One cannot expect children to look after their toys if they have nowhere to keep them. A book case or a wall pocket for picture books is a *must* for a child. There are so many inexpensive paperback editions (children's Picture Puffins, Faber paperbacks and others) that every child should be able to build up a library of really worthwhile books. All young children, too, should be taken with their mothers to the nearest Public Library. Most of them nowadays have a good selection of picture books which can be borrowed.

Looking at picture books, hearing stories read and told by mothers and fathers is something which children enjoy tremendously, and once begun it generally proves so worthwhile it becomes a family tradition.

As parents watch their children at play they themselves will think of new ideas and things for them to do. Special times like Christmas, Easter, Hallowe'en, Saint Valentine's Day, etc. have their own ways of being celebrated. There is certainly nothing so satisfying as to see one's children, even in a small and poky room, really happily absorbed in their play.

Simple recipes for the home :
Home-made finger paint. One needs to beat together, $\frac{1}{2}$ a cup of soap flakes (not a powder or detergent), $\frac{1}{2}$ cup of instant cold water starch and $\frac{5}{8}$ of a cup of water; the mixture should be of the consistency of whipped potatoes; food colouring can be added. A formica or plastic table top can be used if the children do not want to keep their paintings, otherwise shiny shelf paper; wipe a wet sponge over the surface, i.e. table top or paper first, spoon out the paint with a plastic spoon.
Dough. 2 cups of flour, 1 cup of salt, 1 cup of water with food colouring in it and two tablespoonfuls of cooking oil, then knead these all together until they reach a nice consistency.
Papier-mâché. Make some cold-water paste in a large bowl or bucket. Tear up newspaper about the size of a postage stamp and then stir into the paste. The whole mass should become a grey putty-like substance. It shouldn't be too wet. It can be modelled like clay and when it has dried and hardened can be varnished and painted.

17

Play in the nursery and infant school

A thousand mile journey begins with the first steps

Chinese Proverb

Many of us would feel that apart from the home the best place for play for the child between two and five years of age is the Nursery School or Class which in essence should provide exactly the same facilities and staffing, even though it will be part of the Infant School to which it is attached.

The Nursery School has often been called an extension of the home, and is certainly not a substitute for it, and the close relationship that exists between the Nursery School staff and the family does mean that both work together for the wellbeing of the child concerned.

There is always a feeling of welcome to whoever brings the child along. Mothers often linger to talk and watch their child after having helped him off with his outdoor things, and so they get a chance to see what is going on, the play facilities available, what their child enjoys, and his contact with others.

Here, a mother may meet other mothers, perhaps neighbours she has never actually spoken to or ones that come from farther away. This enlarges her world of social relationships, friendships develop and the children may go to each others' homes or meet in the street for play at weekends and in the holidays.

The Nursery School gives the anxious mother support, the busy mother time and the tired mother rest.

One of the great advantages of the Nursery School as compared with the home is that it is purpose-built, with the needs of small children in mind. This means that the furniture and fittings are child-sized, so that boys and girls can do things for themselves and be as independent as they wish.

There should be space both indoors and out, with easy access to a garden and a real one if possible, with grass, trees, mounds, bushes, growing things and paths. Part of the layout should provide a hard surface for use in wet weather.

There is a variety of outdoor equipment which is flexible, imaginative and excellent for children's physical development. Most Nursery Schools are small (they vary from 40 to 120 children) with the children divided into family groups. Some Nursery Schools are part-time, one group of children attending in the mornings and another in the afternoons; others, of course, have children for the full day and provide a mid-day meal. The ages of the children range from two to five, though the proportion of two-year-olds tends to be small.

Some people feel the two-year-old is too young to attend Nursery School, but anyone who has dragged a child of this age wearily round the shops, restrained him at the launderette, kept him quiet in a flat that is not sound-proof or prevented him from running out into the busy street, longs for him to go to one.

Children of this age want to try out all their newly-discovered skills in climbing and running; they want everything within reach and they are eager for the company of other children.

Any well-equipped playroom will contain a wide range of materials—those that enable children to play fully and creatively —and each playroom should provide the full range of activities.

It is not a good idea to have certain activities confined to certain rooms, one having all the messy play, another the large equipment, another the quiet things. This arrangement does not work really successfully. Children like to feel they can find everything they want in their own room with their own teacher. They forget what is available if they cannot see it because it is in another room, and the teacher herself may never be able to watch her children in their quiet play if she happens to have charge of the messy room.

The same thing applies to children from five to seven; they also forget what is available if they cannot actually see it, and they too like to be with their own teacher.

When the children arrive in the morning certain activities will be ready for them; paints mixed or ready for mixing, clay on the clay table where the children can see it, the water play ready and the room looking attractive and gay.

Children need opportunities to go to cupboards and shelves and to choose for themselves what they are going to play with. If activities such as puzzles, fitting toys, paper, crayons, etc., are put out ready for them on the tables they tend to sit down and play with them without making any effort to select something.

This also means that if they have not taken a plaything from the shelves they do not feel any obligation to put it away. This is something we want children to do, to learn to accept responsibility for their own choices and to take care of the materials they use.

Rooms will be arranged so that children get the maximum of value from the possible space; corners made by the use of low shelves, etc., provide cosy playing spaces, a comfortable book corner or one for bricks.

All the activities that have already been mentioned will be available and all sorts of play can spill over into the passages and the easily accessible garden, as boys and girls play indoors or out as they wish, weather, of course, permitting.

Buildings, of course, differ; a Nursery School in a converted house may have all kinds of small rooms where children can play and even climb stairs. There is generally a special period of music and story, otherwise children need long spells of spontaneous and uninterrupted play. Time is 'child's time' and not that of the busy, hurrying adult world.

Whatever routines there are—washing perhaps before dinner if a mid-day meal is provided, a rest time, clearing up, etc. are reduced to a minimum, but children are expected to accept them and understand why they are necessary.

Leaving mother for the first time can be a traumatic experience for a young child, who, because he has no sense of time believes his beloved parent has gone for ever when she walks out of the Nursery School door.

We want to make children's first social relationships outside the home happy and satisfying ones, and so that a child does not feel lost and rejected his first visit to Nursery School will probably be short and his mother will stay with him.

Gradually, as the days go by, he will stay longer, mother will leave him for short periods, perhaps to go shopping. Then will come the day, sooner or later, when he no longer needs her, he has settled happily in his new environment.

Some children settle much more quickly than others. A few may have to be left at once without this slow transition from home to school if circumstances make it impossible for a mother or other member of the family to stay. Five-year-old children joining a reception class in an Infant School need this same gradual settling-in process if mother or someone from home can manage it.

The skilled teacher will be in charge of a group of about 20 or 25 children, with perhaps two girls who are taking their Nursery Nurses Certificate, or an older person who has already obtained this qualification, to help her provide guidance and security, to give and receive love.

This setting is planned for the child. It is an environment where emotional outlets are provided for and understood, where intellectual and social experiences are made available through play, where a child is both an individual and a member of a group, where he is able to develop in his own way and at his own pace.

What of play in the Infant School?

All sorts of phrases are bandied about nowadays—free activity, the integrated day, family or vertical grouping, team teaching, and often no one knows what they mean.

Children come home from school and when parents ask what they have been doing all day they murmur 'playing,' and there is a dreadful feeling that they cannot possibly be learning anything at all.

In the old days when a teacher stood up in front of the class all day and talked at the children it seemed so much safer. Surely the children were having valuable information stuffed into their heads? However, because boys and girls are all sitting still and appearing to listen it does not necessarily mean they are; we can be present in body but miles away in our dreams.

Children are individuals all at different stages, 'all with their own special needs and problems even within a certain development age-span. We know they learn best when they are interested and see the reason behind the skills they are acquiring, and they learn by doing and finding out things for themselves.

Many teachers of children under eight now start the day with a period, first thing in the morning (very occasionally in the afternoon), for what is generally called free activity, creative play, or free choice. This means that children can choose what to play with from the many activities there in the classroom, and all the materials that the good Nursery School has—a home corner, book corner, bricks, clay, painting, etc.—are provided. After perhaps an hour of this kind of play the children may be gathered together for more formal groups for reading, writing and number work.

Sometimes, there is a discussion after the free-activity period, when children talk about the things they have been doing. This may then be linked with their reading, writing and number activities; sometimes, however, there is no link between the two at all. There will, of course, be time during the day for listening to stories and poetry and for Music and Movement.

If teachers start off with a free-play period they often want to go further and have an integrated day. As the word implies, play and work, as it were, spill over into each other and it is difficult sometimes to discover where one begins and the other ends. The children are not concerned with dividing their learning into neat, watertight compartments; it follows the line of their own interests and needs.

Before the integrated day can become a reality the teacher will know her children and have created a happy and secure atmosphere and planned her room carefully with the sort of materials the children will need and enjoy using.

There will be plenty of books, charts, lists, pictures, etc., that the children can consult, reading books they can tackle as well as attractive picture books. There will be all sorts of stimulating things that encourage learning—cooking recipes with the ingredients at hand, waste material of all kinds, word games, number games, woodwork, water with plenty of things for measuring, writing and weighing materials.

Children may start the day, not with actual play but with some reading or writing they want to do, but this will be by their own choice. They may go on to paint, make a model with a group of other children, play in the home corner or use some number apparatus.

Each child, however, needs to feel that what he is doing is meaningful for him, and he quite naturally links his play and his learning together. This is what is happening all the time at all levels of development.

The teacher may challenge him with an idea, throw out a suggestion or an enrichment for the piece of work he is doing which he may follow with enthusiasm. Obviously, some children will be slower and less imaginative than others, and may need more help and encouragement.

The freer the children are to work and play at their own rate the more difficult it is for the teacher who needs to use the children's own interests to introduce them to the techniques of reading, writing and number, or to know what stage each child is at and when a suggestion from her or a specific bit of teaching is needed and will be accepted and understood.

The children should move freely about the room, talking to each other and there should be no demand that work and play be separated into different parts of the day.

Many teachers working on the integrated day not only have no break themselves, but find the children do not want an official playtime either. Milk is drunk when a child wants it, and if the classroom has easy access to the playground or garden children can run out freely if they wish.

Obviously a good building can help enormously the many activities the children want to enjoy : a sink where water is easily obtainable, room for storing, and places where children can exhibit what they have done. Some new schools are built on what is called the 'open plan' system. This gives easy communication between classes; teachers and children are not imprisoned behind doors and yet if two classes are, as it were, linked together there will probably be some form of division between them so that teachers and children do not interfere with each other, and there is a feeling that children belong to their own teacher.

Most good Infants' Schools are bursting with evidence of interesting activities, beautiful paintings and collages that the children have done, interesting stories that they have written and models they have made.

Another fairly recent innovation at the Infant School stage is family or vertical grouping. This means that children of five, six, and seven are all together in the same class. Sometimes this pattern is varied by having the sevens on their own and the fives and sixes together.

This sort of grouping is one that the village school has often had to contend with, but now it is sometimes done by choice. Its advantages are that children are not being constantly moved to make way for new entrants, that members of the same family and friends can be in the same class if they so wish and that the teacher has not got too many children at the same stage, all demanding the same kind of help and attention. The older children often help and encourage the younger ones and it leads them to be thoughtful and loving towards their weaker brethren. The system has its disadvantages. Sometimes the younger children are a nuisance, demanding too much from the older ones, or clinging to brothers and sisters.

It is obvious that the teacher must have a very flexible day as the fives will certainly not be ready to do the things the older children enjoy and they must not be fobbed off with meaningless occupations just to keep them busy while the older children are attended to. The day must, in fact, be an integrated one with everyone playing and working at their own rate, and the younger children must have their fair share of attention with plenty of materials they enjoy using.

It may be necessary to divide the children for story and music, one teacher taking the five- to six-year-olds, another the sevens, as the younger ones will probably need something a little different.

It is very important, if vertical grouping is used, that the seven-year-olds are really stretched. It is only too easy for them to become bored if the environment is planned mainly for the younger children. Many teachers are finding that the seven-year-olds do better if they are on their own and a change of teacher at six plus can be quite stimulating.

As with every method, it is the enthusiasm of the teacher that makes it a success; some teachers welcome vertical grouping, others do not care for it and so, with them, it is less successful.

We often talk about 'permissiveness' in schools as if it was a dangerous thing. *The Concise Oxford Dictionary* defines it as 'giving permission,' and this in itself is very commendable. Children are given permission to work at their own rate, and in their own time, and to choose how they work. This makes the whole process of learning interesting and exciting and children very soon meet the discipline that any activity in work or play sets them because of its own nature and purpose. Nor should we believe that children do not want to learn; they long to be able to manage their own environment and to understand the world of people and things which they are meeting every day.

Permissiveness does not mean hitting your playmate over the head with a hammer, spoiling his painting, or breaking his new engine. Education is as deeply concerned with good relationships as it is with learning to read. Nor does permissiveness mean that children are simply messing about doing nothing, running around, shouting, being rough and careless with the equipment, spilling paint, splashing water at each other and generally misbehaving. No one would give children permission to behave in this way nor do they really enjoy it.

'Our teacher's daft,' said a small six year old, 'she lets the kids throw things about and shout and be cheeky,' and she sighed deeply over the strange behaviour of grown-ups.

The active classroom is a hive of industry, children getting on with their own work or play, sharing information, talking and helping each other with no feeling of competition as each is working and playing at his own optimum rate.

The temptation to spend money on mechanical gadgets to teach children things they can often learn just as effectively through their own interests and activities must be avoided. It is sad to think of the expensive equipment some schools for older children have invested in, locked away in cupboards because no one has the time, the space, or even the knowledge to use it.

A rich environment indoors and out, space, a wise and skilful teacher, and small classes so that children can receive the individual care and attention that they need, is what is wanted.

18

Conclusions

The days that make us happy make us wise

ANON.

It has taken a very long time to discover childhood as a separate entity.

In the process of being discovered children have been at the mercy of the society and age in which they have been born and because they are small, weak and helpless they are powerless to do anything against the adult world.

Even today strange things are done, supposedly for their general wellbeing. New gadgets of all kinds are tried out on unsuspecting boys and girls. In America parents are told they can raise their child's I.Q. and give their baby of 21 months a reading vocabulary of 160 words by following a given book of instructions.

There is at present much talk about 'compensatory education' and the Social Science Research Council has given £175,000 for the development of special pre-school programmes for compensatory education.

Professor Bernstein feels[1] that the term compensatory education is a curious one for a number of reasons, 'I do not understand,' he says, 'how we can talk about compensatory education to children, who in the first place have not yet been offered an adequate educational environment.'

There is even talk in some quarters that too much time is given to play.

So young children's rights still need safeguarding. The money spent on Nursery School and Class accommodation is lamentably small; the ordinary flat or home is rarely built or planned with the needs of young children in mind.

It is far more difficult to get lodgings of any kind if there are young children.

So often, if a child is ill-treated and neglected it is either because the parents suffered in the same kind of way and are, themselves, desperately ineffectual and disturbed and so have nothing to give, or are living under conditions which have driven them past bearing.

It is platitudinous to say that the children of today are the adults of tomorrow, but nevertheless it is true, and if we find some of the young people of today aggressive, hostile, difficult and destructive, there is no one one to blame except ourselves and the society in which they have grown up.

As has been stressed in previous chapters, children have a right to their childhood, they did not ask to be born and so one might well say they owe us nothing.

Play is their way of growing and learning, of coming to terms with life and discovering themselves and their environment. It gives them intense delight and this should be sufficient justification in itself.

Boys and girls do not play in a vacuum and the wise love and understanding of their parents and the quality of acceptance and affection they receive is equally important. Perhaps most of us would agree with Henry Vaughan when he said :

> Quickly would I make my path even
> And by mere playing go to heaven.

APPENDICES

Safety in toys

Rattles that break easily when banged, exposing small objects (beads, peas etc.) that can be easily swallowed, should not be given to small babies. A rattle should be easy to hold and should have good colours, innocuous filling and no sharp edges; it should be light in case the baby hits himself and stout enough not to fall to pieces.

Children should *not* be given :

plastic objects that break or come apart, exposing sharp edges that can cut;

cuddly woolly toys stuffed with dirty and unhygienic materials, e.g. fluff which can be easily removed, sucked and swallowed; toys with eyes that can be pulled out; dolls and animals whose arms and legs can easily be detached and have sharp wires;

paint that can be sucked and contains poisonous elements (the British Standard Institution recommends that painted finish should not contain more than 1.1 per cent lead); mouth organs and toys which are meant to be sucked and do not have insoluble colouring;

celluloid toys which are inflammable; electrical toys—even for the older child—which are rated at more than 20 volts with their transformers;

wooden toys that are nailed instead of screwed so that, when prised apart, they are dangerous;

plastic bags which young children can unwittingly put over their heads, so suffocating themselves;

artificial ponds, paddling pools or tubs of water into which very young children can, if unsupervised, fall and drown;

slides with metal surfaces which if left too long in even ordinary direct sunlight can become very hot and cause friction burns;

cheap tools with blades which snap, handles which come off, pincers with nail removing prongs which can puncture a child's face when the nail is suddenly removed (softwood is needed at the woodwork bench, otherwise children cannot get the nails into the wood to make anything);

empty hair-spray containers which when empty are particularly dangerous when exposed to heat or punctured.

Tricycles should be regarded as vehicles and have their brakes tested and be oiled regularly. Chain-guards should not be disposed of if they become detached. If, as on some models, the chain is very close to the pedals, a child's sock can become caught, and if he is riding fast he can be pitched over the handlebars.

Friction cars should have their cogs protected as young children tend to put them to their mouths to feel the vibrations, and so cut their tongues and lips.

Trucks, cots and prams, if large enough for children to sit in, should be strong enough to hold them and sufficiently well balanced not to tip up. Otherwise, they should be too small for the child to try.

Baby walkers should be steady, and should not run so freely that a child falls on its face.

Garden and indoor swings should not be placed in such a position that a child has to run in front of them to reach some other part of the playroom or garden. Swings should always be in a safe place, out of the way of general play.

When babies and young children are playing in private homes, electric fittings into which pencils, small fingers, etc., can be poked, or switches that can easily be reached and switched on, should be guarded. The same applies to spin-dryers and refrigerators into which children can crawl. If old refrigerators are used to play in, the doors should be removed. Guards should always protect open, gas or electric fires.

Old motor cars or other similar vehicles (delightful for imaginative play) often have heavy doors that can be slammed, pinching children's fingers. These doors are best removed.

Firework displays should always be very carefully supervised and children not allowed to play with and light fireworks on their own. They do not realize their potential dangers, but put them into bottles which explode, throw them about or light them in a dangerous manner.

Play for the sick child

Many children who are not very ill would be happier if their cot or bed were moved down to the kitchen close to mother where they can watch what is going on and have her within easy reach.

A favourite doll or cuddly toy who can share in the treatment the child is having, e.g. an injection or pill, has a comforting effect.

A large tray is useful on which can be kept all the oddments the child is playing with : paper, scissors, pencils, crayons, writing-paper etc.

Other useful items for the child ill in bed include :

things to sort and thread, tidy or match, shells, beads, old Christmas cards, playing cards, sticky paper and old magazines are enjoyed; so are novelties which are unfamiliar such as a snowstorm, Japanese flowers which come out in water, a musical box, a magnifying glass;

screwtop jars, little boxes whose lids can be taken on and off are fun, and lots of empty cardboard boxes into which can be swept all sorts of unwanted bits or the toys that are not being played with; bags or baskets which can be attached to the bed or cot are useful to keep within easy reach the toys a child may want to use;

glove puppets, dolls with clothes to dress or undress, bits of material to wrap round the doll, tiny dolls and dolls' furniture which can be arranged in old shoe boxes like a dolls' house, cardboard dolls which can be dressed in their paper clothes;

little cars, lorries, etc., which a child can play with on his tray. running them up and down, small boxes of bricks, village sets, garage and farm sets, etc.;

simple fitting toys, puzzles, mosaics, sewing cards;

colouring books, not really a creative play material for the well child, are suitable for the child who easily tires; so are 'rub off' and 'cut out' pictures;

picture books, i.e. some small ones that are not too heavy to hold; a new one, some familiar ones;

dough or modelling wax : something with which the child can model if he so wishes;

if the bed or cot is by a wall a large sheet of black or brown paper, or even newspaper on which he can draw with chalks is useful, also a mirror so placed that a child can see what is happening outside in the garden or street;

mobiles to watch and a little bell to ring if the adult is needed help to make a child feel he is not cut off from the world, if he has to be left alone;

a flannelgraph and all the pieces that go with it.

Children want to be read to and played with and games like ludo, snakes and ladders and Happy Families keep mother or his friends near him.

It must be remembered that children who are ill :
tire more easily,
find concentration more difficult,
play at a younger age level than normally,
need extra affection and understanding,
often need distracting and amusing,
do not want complicated toys to play with or those composed of lots of small awkward pieces that will get lost in the bed.

Any of the play material suggested on the longer list that a parent feels she can allow has all sort of possibilities, but it is better to provide simple things with love and patience than the more involved and messy ones if they are going to cause exasperation and anger.

Fathers are important to the sick child. Their firmness and strength can be reassuring to a frightened and worried child.

Suggested play materials for young children

Painting
Powder paints in a variety of colours—i.e. vermilion, lemon yellow, crimson lake, light red, Prussian or turquoise blue, yellow ochre, emerald green, purple. Black and white should be included.

Some children—the older ones—may like to mix their own colours. The powder paint can then be put dry into patty-pans. If the paint is already mixed for the children it should have the consistency of salad cream.

Paper
Large sheets of paper—sometimes children like different shapes, such as circles, triangles, etc., and different colours—black for example. Children don't mind using newspaper if one is short of painting paper.

Brushes
Size 10–12 is a useful size for the nursery children, though other sizes are valuable too. It is often a good idea to provide children with a separate brush for each colour.

Finger Painting
Cold water paste coloured with powder paint, should be nice and thick—large sheets of non-absorbent paper (just wipe a damp sponge over it first) or oilcloth for very young children who do not want to keep their finished products.

Children need large dollops of paint with more than one colour. They want to be able to use their fingers, hands, arms, fists, knuckles, etc.

Crayons
Large crayons in bright colours, pastels sometimes tend to be rather messy for young children.

Charcoals, pencils, felt pens (some children love using a biro); older children often like pen and ink and the greater variety of materials children have available to draw with the better.

Clay
Clay is much better than plasticine, as children can really have large pieces, and it does not get dirty. Can be kept in a plastic bag in a large biscuit tin or special bin. Cheap to buy, even if a little more trouble is needed in keeping it in the right condition.

Dough
Flour and cooking salt mixed with water so that it is pliable but not sticky (recipe p. 137), can be coloured with vegetable dyes. Blocks of salt for carving—children can use a suitable tool i.e. a spoon, a clay modelling tool or a small blunt knife or spatula.

Sand
Apart from the outdoor sandpit, dry silver sand is pleasant to play with in a large sink, bowl or bath. It runs through the fingers a little like water. Things for filling and pouring needed. If no outdoor sandpit is available, a really large sand tray or sand trolley should be provided for the children to dig in.

Water play
Specially-made water table, large bath, old sink, bowls, with a variety of things to use, e.g. things to fill and empty, i.e. jars, bottles of different sizes, jugs, teapots, funnels, tubing, sponges, sieves, boats, fountain pen fillers, objects that float and sink etc. There are all sorts of plastic containers now available which can be used in water play.

Sand and Water
Children get a great deal of satisfaction in mixing sand and water. Sometimes this is only possible out of doors in summer, but two large trays, one with sand and one with water next to each other, invite mixing.

Bricks
Bricks of all sizes and shapes, large wooden blocks, pieces of flat wood for roofs, small cars, lorries, etc., of all kinds. A passage or a corner for brick building so that children can play undisturbed is very useful.

Domestic Play
Dolls, doll's bed with bedclothes and clothes and wraps for the dolls, china and plastic dolls. Pastry sets and pastry making.

Wendy House
There is really no need to have an elaborate exterior, as it is what is in the Wendy House that matters, and in a small room an elaborate wooden structure takes up so much room. Two simple screens are quite adequate. Inside one wants things such as table, chairs, dresser, stove, teasets, table cloths, brushes, dusters, large bed, and all the bits and pieces which make up a home—a telephone, an iron, pans for the stove. It should not be too elaborate or it leaves nothing to the children's imagination. A telephone outside the Wendy House is useful too.

Children sometimes find an adult easy chair or couch rather pleasant to have in the nursery itself, but this will depend on the size of one's playroom and the space available.

Hospital Corner
Bed with blanket, toy stethoscope, bandages, etc. for child to play doctors, nurses, hospitals, etc.

Dressing-up Clothes
Skirts, hats, beads, flowers, veils, cloaks, busman's and fireman's outfit, etc., dressing-up clothes which will appeal to the boys are particularly important.

Doll's Washing
Rubber dolls, wooden dolls, with bowls of water, towels to dry the dolls, soap, etc. Mangle, clothes horse, bowl, soap, clothes pegs, things to wash.

Scrubbing
This is difficult in one room, as one does not want the floor to get wet, but children can often scrub the passages, the cloakroom, steps, etc., outside—bucket, scrubbing brush, soap, apron.

Indoors and Out
Farm sets, traffic sets, small dolls and dolls' furniture, pastry sets, puzzles, pegboards, hammer-toys, constructional and fitting toys, beads, posting boxes, picture matching, scissors, coloured paper, paste, etc.

Waste Material
Cotton reels, cartons, bobbins, spools from films, cardboard rolls, cardboard, string, pipe cleaners, date boxes, wheels, etc. The under-five is not so ingenious with waste material as the five to seven and will obviously need more help.

Woodwork
Bench vice, saws, pincers, hammers, screwdriver (a two-inch blade), sawing blocks, nails, screws, sandpaper. Soft wood in different shapes and sizes from timber yards, furniture factories, etc.

Books Corner
Books can be in a wall pocket if space is limited. For list of suitable books, see NSA leaflet.

Children's SCIENTIFIC INTERESTS can be stimulated by such things as magnets, compasses, spirit levels, egg-timers, magnifying glasses, bicycle pumps, locks, pulleys, cranes, clocks, spring balances, old TV set or radio (for detailed list see *Scientifiic Interests in the Primary School*, NFF, 2/-).

Children's interests in NATURE can be encouraged by plants, flowers, pets, collections of such things as pebbles, shells, feathers, etc.

A Music Corner
A music corner with percussion instruments, chime bells, dulcimer etc. can have its value but its is sometimes of more interest to the young child to integrate music with other play, i.e. a tambourine, or triangle with the dressing up clothes, some flags with the drums or bells etc. A gramophone and suitable records are enjoyed by the children (see NSA leaflet of suggested records).

Out of Doors
Suggestions, depending on space : boxes, planks, ladders, ropes, old tyres, trestles, tree trunks, swing, slide, a jungle gym, commando nets, bars, low walls for walking on, steps, little outdoor house, pipes for crawling through, grassy mounds, bushes. An old car, a cart or boat is grand for play; it should, however, be made safe for use, i.e. fingers can be trapped in heavy doors. Wagons, cars, bikes, trolleys, prams, ropes, hoops, etc.

Sandpit
Buckets, spades, things to fill and empty. If the nursery has a garden,

little forks, trowels and watering cans are useful, but the forks and trowels should be kept for the garden—they can be dangerous if used rather freely in the sandpit.

Local shops should always be approached for waste material—such things as small pieces of material used in upholstery, cardboard cartons, wood, scraps of leather, fur, etc., are often thrown away and could well be used by the children.

A shop is really not a Nursery School interest though they enjoy large empty boxes and cartons to load onto carts and trolleys. It is more suitable for the five- to seven-year-olds.

Advantage should be taken of special occasions. Festivals, such as Christmas and Easter when presents and decoration Easter Eggs can be made. Hallowe'en, and Guy Fawkes, making snowmen, children's birthdays, planting bulbs, making grass houses and playing in the newly-cut grass can be great fun. If members of staff have to go to the bank, post office, supermarket, etc., and one or two children can go, too, they always enjoy it.

The older nursery children can sometimes visit a nearby place of interest—the fire station, bus depot, railway station, park, etc.

Firms which supply play materials and equipment

Abbatt, Paul and Marjorie, Ltd., 94 Wimpole Street, London w1
    Play material, large play equipment
Adventure Playthings, Queensway, Glenrothes, Fife, Scotland, and
Kemp House, 154/158 City Road, London wc1
    Play materials, large play equipment
Arnold, E. J. & Son, 12 Butterly Street, Leeds 10, Yorks.
    Play materials, large play equipment
Camphill Schools, Botton Village, Danby, near Whitby, Yorks.
    Bricks, dolls, lorries, furniture by mentally defective boys
Copthorn Woodcraft Studios, Colne Road, Coggleshall, Essex
    Constructional toys
Crowdy's Wood Products, The Old Bakery, Clanfield, Oxon.
    Building and fitting toys, rattles, etc.
Crowther, Frank, Ltd., 410 Brightside Lane, Sheffield, Yorks.
    Agility and large play equipment
Dryad Handicrafts Ltd., Northgates, Leicester
    Play material and handicraft materials of all kinds
Educational Supply Association, Pinnacles, Harlow, Essex
    Play materials, musical instruments, furniture, etc.
Elliot, Louise, Bridgers Farmhouse, Hurstpierpoint, Sussex
    Do it yourself rag dolls & toys, ready for cutting out and making
Escor Toys, Purewell, Christchurch, Hants.
    Wooden toys beautifully carved and finished
France, James (Toys) Ltd., 7 Gun Street, Reading, Berks.
    Children's books and toys
Furnitures Associated Products, 142 Humber Road, London se3
    Large play equipment (Superla)
Galt, James, Brookfield Road, Cheadle, Cheshire, and 30 Great
Marlborough Street, London w1
    Play material, large play equipment, furniture, etc.
Good-Wood Toys, (Lavant), Department ns11, Lavant, Chichester,
Sussex
    Large play material

Hamley's, 200–202 Regent Street, London w1
   Toys and play material of all kinds
Hope, Thomas, & Hudson Sankey Ltd., Ashton Mill,
Chapeltown Street, Manchester, M12 NH
   Play material and large equipment
Jamie Toys, Cross Street, Polegate, Sussex
   Wooden toys and play material
Kaye Toys, Brookfield Road, Bristol 6
   Large play equipment
Kiddiecraft Ltd., 3 Lower Road, Kenley, Surrey
   Hilary Page Toys
Mann Egerton, Cromer Road, Norwich, Norfolk
   Wooden tables and chairs
Play and Learn, 144 High Street, Maidenhead, Berks.
   Toys of all kinds
Philip and Tacey, Northants, Andover, Hampshire
   Play and handwork materials of all kinds, furniture
School Utilities, Church Street, Romford, Essex
   Play material (also made to special requirements)
Self, Vera, The Butterfly, Gt. Finborough, near Stowmarket
Suffolk
   Hand-made soft toys
Tiger Toys, Durford Mill, Petersfield, Hants.
   Play material and wooden toys
Tratman, Lowther, Ltd., 19/21 Broad Quay, Bristol
   Large play equipment
Tridias, 8 Savill Row, Bath, Somerset
   Toys of all kinds
Whittle, R. W. Ltd., P.V. Works, Monton, Manchester, Lancs.
   Large play equipment and climbing nets, tubular furniture
Wicksteeds, Mendip Works, Royston, Herts.
   Agility and large play equipment
Woodpecker Toys, Mill Lane, Stourbridge, Worcs.
   Bricks, sets of animals and small vehicles in wood
Wynter, Susan, 31 Onslow Gardens, London N12
   Moving wooden toys, Noah's Arks, etc.

Books
Alan Tucker Children's Bookshop, Station Approach, Stroud, Glos.
The Angel Bookshop, 102 Islington High Street, London w1
B. H. Blackwell Ltd., Oxford

Bookland and Co. Ltd., Old Custom House Building, 70 Watergate, Chester

Book One, 23 Temple Fortune Parade, Finchley Road, London NW11

Bowes & Bowes Ltd., 1/2, Trinity Street, Cambridge

Chelsea Book Shop, 289 King's Road, London SW3
    Picture books and story books of all kinds

Children's Book Centre Ltd, 140 Kensington Church Street, London W8

Children's Bookshop, Cirencester, Glos.

Children's Bookshop, 34 High Street, Banbury, Oxon.

Domino, Beckenham

E. & W. Fielder Ltd., 54 Hill Road, Wimbledon

Don Gresswell Ltd., Bridge House, Grange Park, London N21

Harrod's Ltd., Knightsbridge, London SW1

Hammick's Bookshop, Downing Street, Farnham, Surrey

Heffer's Bookshop, Cambridge

Midland Education Ltd., Market Street, Leicester

Owl and the Pussy Cat, 11 Flask Walk, Hampstead, London NW3
    Picture and story books and toys

Rainbow Bookshop, 27b Bridge Street, Walton-on-Thames

Sisson & Parker Ltd., Wheelergate, Nottingham

Thin's Bookshop, Edinburgh

Periodicals concerned with children's books
Books for your Children, Anne Wood, 14, Stoke Road, Guildford, Surrey

Lane, East Aldershot, Hampshire (four issues a year)

Growing Point, Margery Fisher, Ashton Manor, Northampton (nine issues a year)

The Junior Bookshelf, Marsh Hall, Thurstonland, Huddersfield, Yorks (six issues a year)

Children's Book Review, Five Owls Press Ltd., 67, High Street, Wormley, Broxbourne, Herts. (six issues a year)

Films on play

NURSERY SCHOOL FILMS

Title	Origin & Date	Size	Silent or Sound	Black & white or colour	Runni Time
A Day in a Nursery School	Berkshire 1958	16mm	Sound		21 min
Childhood, Right of Every Child	Italy 1960	16mm	Sound	B & W	30 min
The Adult in the Small Child's world	1960	16mm	Sound	B & W	35 mins
Play and Personality	Cassel Hospital 1960	16mm	Sound	B & W	20 mins
The Time of their Lives	1962	16mm	Sound	B & W	30 mins

oduced by	Available from	Comments
	Berkshire Edn. Authority, Shire Hall, Reading, Berks	A quite interesting little film, but should be shown by someone who understands what the nursery school stands for, and can clarify certain points in it.
chmied	Concord Films Council, Nacton, Ipswich.	This is one of three films made by Mrs Goldschmied.
chmied	Concord Films Council, Nacton Ipswich	This film illustrates varied activities enjoyed by children between 10 months–3 years in a play group, indicating the role of the adult responsible in guiding and encouraging them in play.
el ital	Edric Films Ltd., 34–36 Oak End Way, Gerrards Cross, Bucks	An excellent film with a very good commentary taken at the Cassel Hospital, showing a group of nursery aged children whose mothers are receiving treatment. The children's problems as shown in their play reflect those of their mothers.
nal ation	Concord Films Council, Nacton, Ipswich	This film illustrates children in an American Nursery School and how they learn through play. Each game or activity will be of some value to their development, but for them it is all fun.

Title	Origin & Date	Size	Silent or Sound	Black & white or colour	Running Time
A Place to Play	Bristol & District Nursery Play Groups Association	16mm	Sound	Colour	30 mins
It's Mine	Poland 1968	16mm	Sound	B & W	25 mins
Springs of Learning	GB 1967	16mm	Sound	B & W	30 mins
Children growing up	U.K. 1972	16mm	Sound	Colour	25 mins
Exploring Novelty	GB 1967	16mm	Sound	B & W	10 mins
Child in a Glass Ball	GB 1968	16mm	Sound	B & W	14 mins
Autistic Children	U.K. 1970	16mm	Sound	B & W	25 mins
Happy Adventure	Graphic 1965	16mm	Sound	B & W	30 mins

roduced by	Available from	Comments
	Eric Walker Concord Films Council, Nacton, Ipswich, Suffolk	Illustrates the lack of play space and the way in which play groups can help—shots of a Nursery School. Illustrate standards of play.
	Concord Films Council, Nacton, Ipswich	Sub-titles in English. Shows 2, 3 & 4-year-old children in a Polish Nursery School.
? TV	Foundation Film Library	A series of 6 films. Excellent shots and useful commentary on the early years. Babyhood, rising 2. Ideas of their own, etc.
? TV	A. R. Crafts BBC. TV Enterprises Villiers House The Broadway London W5 2PA England (for sale or hire)	A series of 5 films on children up to 5+ showing the way they develop. There is a second series of 5 colour films on children from 5+ to puberty on roughly the same lines as the first series though taking the form of an inquiry.
k Hospitals Children	British Film Institute	Shows the response of a 3-, 5- & 6-year-old boy to a new object when left alone to play.
don School ilm hnique	Concord Films Council, Nacton, Ipswich, Suffolk	A very sincere film which is a study of autistic children, their problems and methods of teaching.
	Concord Films Council Nacton Ipswich IP10 0JZ Suffolk	A useful film showing the behaviour and play problems of autistic children.
ional on of chers	Central Film Library, Government Bldg., Bromyard Avenue w3	A useful film, concerned with young children at school.

CHILD DEVELOPMENT

Title	Origin & Date	Size	Silent or Sound	Black & white or colour	Running Time
He Acts his Age (Ages and Stages Series)	Canada 1949	16mm	Sound	Colour	14 mins
The Terrible Twos and the Trusting Threes	Canada 1950	16mm	Sound	Colour	22 mins
The Frustrating Fours and Fascinating Fives	Canada 1952	16/35mm	Sound	Colour	22 mins
From Sociable Six to Noisy Nine (Ages and Stages)	Canada 1953	16mm	Sound	Colour	21 mins
Seven Up	Granada TV 1964	16mm	Sound	B & W	30 mins

Produced by	*Available from*	*Comments*
tional m rd of nada	Central Film Library, Government Bldg., Bromyard Ave., w3	This is the first film in the Ages and Stages Series. A pleasant if somewhat superficial film. The colour is uneven, but the shots of children are attractive. It stresses briefly the normal stages through which children pass.
cional m rd of ada	Central Film Library, Government Bldg., Bromyard Ave., w3	The second film in the Ages and Stages Series showing children of 2 and 3 years of age in groups playing in nursery school. Pleasant, though situations are over-simplified and family relationships omitted.
ional m rd of ada	Central Film Library, Government Bldg., Bromyard Ave., w3	A study of the behaviour of 4- and 5-year-old children, both at home and in nursery school. These are the same children who were seen in the previous film (*The Terrible Twos and Trusting Threes*). The shots of the children are lively and spontaneous, though the group play of the 5-year-olds is a little formal.
wley ns Ltd. National Film rd of ada	Central Film Library, Government Bldg., Bromyard Ave., w3	This shows typical behaviour in children of 6 to 9. It is taken in the well-favoured home and deals sensibly with superficial problems without really getting beneath the surface, or coping with family relationships.
nada	Granada TV, 36 Golden Square, w1 and 3 Deansgate, Manchester 3	Spontaneous answers to questions, particularly from children of 7 years of age, appeared on ITV programme.

Title	Origin & Date	Size	Silent or Sound	Black & white or colour	Running Time
Larry	Eire 1960	16mm	Sound	B & W	30 mins
Children who Draw Pictures	Japan 1956	16mm	Sound	B & W	30 mins

PLAY

Title	Origin & Date	Size	Silent or Sound	Black & white or colour	Running Time
A Child Went Forth	USA 1941	16/35mm	Sound	B & W	20 mins
Adventure Playgrounds	GB 1957	16mm	Sound	Colour	15 mins
Children's Playground In Europe	Europe 1961	16mm	Sound	Colour	25 mins
New Playgrounds		16mm	Sound	B & W	13 mins

Produced by	*Available from*	*Comments*
	British Film Institute, 81 Dean St., w1	This film is based on the book *My Oedipus Complex* and is a dramatized account (produced for TV) of a young boy's father—when he comes back from war.
zo chi	Concord Films Council, Nacton, Ipswich	This film is Japanese, with English commentary, illustrating the art activities of young children in a Tokyo school. Following different children of differing personalities over the period of a year we learn how children think, feel and develop.
ph ey & n Ferne New k versity	Central Film Library, Government Building, Bromyard Ave., London w3	A film which shows the natural development and play of children (aged about 3 to 6) in the ideal setting of a holiday camp. Beautifully photographed.
ley ield luction Nat. ing ls c.	16–17 Woodside Terrace, Charing Cross, Glasgow c3	Shows children of varying ages freely satisfying their need to construct, create, etc. spontaneously in a permissive yet secure setting.
lable CFL don, gow or liff)	Central Film Library of Wales, 42 Park Place, Cardiff, Wales	This film shows the imaginative development of all sorts of play equipment and the use of space for children and young people throughout Northern Europe. A delightful film.
onal ing l c,	As above, i.e. London, Glasgow or Cardiff	Quite a useful little film.

Title	Origin & Date	Size	Silent or Sound	Black & white or colour	Running Time
Two and a Half	Canada 1964	16mm	Sound	B & W	8 mins
Children at Play	UK 1966	16mm	Sound	B & W	11 mins
One Potato, Two Potato	UK 1958	16mm	Sound	B & W	18 mins
The Singing Street	UK 1952	16mm	Sound	B & W	18 mins
In Touch	UK 1966	16mm	Sound	B & W	13 mins
As the Twig is Bent	New Zealand 1965	16mm	Sound	B & W	20 mins

Produced by	*Available from*	*Comments*
...ada	Canada House Film Library, Canada House, Trafalgar Square, London, w I	This film shows two little girls aged 2½ at play alone on a winter evening.
...C TV	Central Film Library, Glasgow or Cardiff	An excerpt from the TV Programme *Tomorrow's World*. Shows shortage of houses and two types of play space: the adventure playground and the more conventional type. Good technically, but very short.
	British Film Institute, 81 Dean Street, w I (hire)	London children amusing themselves in the street and playground, playing both traditional and contemporary games. A pleasant, useful little film though at times some of the games are not very suitable to the ages of the children playing them.
	British Film Institute, 81 Dean Street, w I (hire)	The songs and games of children of a variety of ages in Edinburgh. This is an amateur film and the background of the Edinburgh streets is a little dour. It has, however, a pleasing, spontaneous quality. Quite an interesting and lively film.
	Concord Films	Students who are training to work with ineducable children are seen in a movement class. The movements of the children and the participation of the students is delightful to watch.
...v Zealand ...ional ...1 Unit	New Zealand House Film Library, 80 Haymarket, sw I	A delightful film with excellent shots of children at play. The commentary is very simple and the children's environment in New Zealand looks idyllic—as compared with conditions in Britain.

THE CARE OF DEPRIVED CHILDREN

Title	Origin & Date	Size	Silent or Sound	Black & white or colour	Running Time
Children of Change	USA 1960	16mm	Sound	B & W	28 mins
Mentally Handicapped Children Growing up. The Booklands Experiment	UK 1960	16mm	Sound	B & W	22 mins
Play & Development	UK 1967	16mm	Sound	Colour	20 mins
Nursery School for the Blind	UK 1969	16mm	Sound	B & W	
The Red Balloon	France c. 1955	16mm	music	Colour	35 mins
Bush Xmas	Australia	16mm	Sound	B & W	1hr 21 m

roduced by	*Available from*	*Comments*
ng »by for US t. of th and cation the adelphia th mittee Mental th Assoc.	British Film Institute, 81 Dean Street, W I	A rather long film concerned with day-centre care for children whose mothers are working, made for an American audience. There are some delightful shots of children at play, and the need for places where children can go instead of roaming the streets is well brought out—useful as a basis for discussion.
ist Unit	National Society for Mentally Handicapped Children, 5, Bulstrode St., W I	This film shows what can be done with a group of handicapped children from the Fountain Hospital, when they are able to live in small groups under the care housemothers can provide, and with suitable and sufficient play material.
ty icil	D. Norris, Essex County Council, Health Dept., 85–89 New London Road, Chelmsford, Essex	This film shows the place of play in the development of young, mentally handicapped children. Moderately successful.
thy ngham mes ertson	Concord Films, Nacton, Ipswich IP10 0JZ Suffolk	An interesting and useful film, enquiries should be made when ordering in relation to the projector which will be used.
rt orisse	Connoisseur Films Ltd, 54–58 Wardour St., W I	A delightful film of a little boy who on his way to school rescues a balloon.
	Rank Film Library 1 Aintree Rd, Perivale, Greenford, Middlesex	A family of Australian children track down a gang of horse thieves. Lovely photography and delightful children.

DEPRIVATION

Title	Origin & Date	Size	Silent or Sound	Black & white or colour	Running Time
Kate Young. Children in Brief Separation	GB 1968	16mm	Sound	B & W	33 mins
Jane Young. Children in Brief Separation	GB 1968	16mm	Sound	B & W	33 mins
John Young. Children in Brief Separation	GB 1968	16mm	Sound	B & W	45 mins
A Two-Year-Old goes to Hospital	GB 1953	16mm	Sound	B & W	45 mins
Going to Hospital with Mother	GB 1958	16mm	Sound	B & W	30 mins

GENERAL EDUCATION

| First Two Years at School | NZ 1950 | 16mm | Sound | B & W | 23 mins |

oduced by	Available from	Comments
s rtson	Tavistock Child Development Research Unit, Tavistock Centre, Belsize Lane, London NW3	No. 1. Kate 2½ in fostercare for 27 days while mother, whom she visits in hospital, has another baby.
s rtson	Tavistock Child Development Research Unit, Tavistock Centre, Belsize Lane, London NW3	The second film in the series showing the effect of a brief separation on a young child.
s rtson	Tavistock Child Development Research Unit, Tavistock Centre, Belsize Lane, London NW3	A very moving film showing the effects of short residential care on John, aged 17 months, in a residential Nursery.
s rtson	Tavistock Institute of Human Relations, Tavistock Centre, Belsize Lane, London NW3	This film illustrates the problem of admitting a young child to hospital. The film shows the reactions of Laura (aged 2½ years) to the absence of her mother, her behaviour when her parents do visit her and her feelings about hospital procedure. An excellent and moving film of immense interest.
s rtson	Tavistock Institute of Human Relations, Tavistock Centre, Belsize Lane, London, NW3	This is a complementary film to a *Two-Year-Old Goes to Hospital*, and shows Sally's reactions when mother goes and stays in the hospital with her. An excellent film. Both films are provided with a guide booklet.
	New Zealand Film Library, Haymarket, SW1	A pleasant, well-planned film with good shots of children's natural response to their environment. A New Zealand mother looks back on her schooling of 25 years ago and contrasts it with what she sees today.

Title	Origin & Date	Size	Silent or Sound	Black & white or colour	Running Time
I want to go to School	UK 1957	16mm	Sound	B & W	30 min

FILM STRIPS WITH DESCRIPTIVE NOTES

Film strip 1 Painting, building, imaginative, nature

Film strip 2 Carpentry, waste materials, books & domestic play

Film strip 3 Water, sand, clay

Excellently produced with delightful shots of spontaneous play (in colour)

Fourteen Filmloops produced by Camera Talks Ltd, 31, North Row, London WIR 2EN.

These film loops supervised by The Nursery School Association, 89 Stanford Street, London SEI (and obtained from them) show various aspects of play; painting, water play, domestic play, outdoor play etc. (standard 8 mm, super 8 mm)

This is an excellent and lively series with useful and helpful notes supplied (can be bought or hired).

Available from Nursery Schools Association, 89 Stamford Street, London SEI

oduced by	*Available from*	*Comments*
onal on of :hers	Central Film Library, Government Bldg., Bromyard Avenue, w3	A useful film, on day-to-day life in a Primary School.

References

CHAPTER 1

1 J. Bowlby, *Maternal Care and Mental Health,* 1951, World Health Organization
2 D. Burlingham and Anna Freud, *Young Children in Wartime,* 1942; *Infants without Families,* 1943
3 James and Joyce Robertson, *Young Children in Brief Separation, No. 1 Kate, No. 2 Jane, No. 3 John,* Tavistock Child Development Research Unit
4 *Your Child from 6 to 12,* US Department of Health, Education and Welfare, 1949
5 Susanna Millar, *The Psychology of Play,* 1968
6 Jean Piaget, *Play, Dreams and Imitation in Childhood,* 1951
7 Susan Isaacs, *Intellectual Growth in Young Children,* 1930; *Social Development in Young Children,* 1933
8 Susan Isaacs, *The Psychological Aspects of Child Development,* 1935, 2nd edition
9 Erik H. Erikson, *Childhood and Society,* 1950
10 Desmond Morris, *The Naked Ape,* 1967

CHAPTER 2

1 R. D. Laing, *The Divided Self,* 1959
2 Anne Frank, *The Diary of a Young Girl,* 1947
3 Richard Hughes, *A High Wind in Jamaica,* 1929

CHAPTER 3

1 Arthur T. Jersild, *Child Psychology*
2 Susan Isaacs, *Social Development in Young Children,* 1933
3 William Golding, *Lord of the Flies,* 1948
4 Laurie Lee, *Cider with Rosie,* 1959

CHAPTER 4

1 Susan Isaacs, *Social Development in Young Children,* 1933
2 Desmond Morris, *The Naked Ape,* 1967

CHAPTER 5

1 William Hazlitt, *Notes on a Journey through France and Italy*, 1862
2 Laurie Lee, *Cider with Rosie*, 1959
3 Edmund Gosse, *Father and Son*
4 I am indebted to Mrs Grubbe of Balham Nursery School for the account of Andrew
5 Frances Tustin, *A Group of Juniors*, 1951
6 Dorothy Burlingham and Anna Freud, *Young Children in Wartime*, 1942

CHAPTER 6

1 Rhoda Kellogg, *Analyzing Children's Art*, 1969
2 Terezin in 1942–44, *Children's Drawings and Poems*
3 Margaret Lowenfeld, *Play in Childhood*, 1935
4 Frank Baines, *Look Towards the Sea*, 1958

CHAPTER 7

1 Lewis Carroll, *Alice Through the Looking Glass*
2 Richard Church, *Under the Bridge*, 1955
3 I am indebted to a former student for this example
4 I am indebted to Mrs Ann Thwaite for this example

CHAPTER 8

1 Home play, or as it is sometimes called play in the Wendy Corner, means that children have, or make, a little house where they can play at being mothers and fathers
2 I am indebted to Mrs Aldous for this observation, from her unpublished thesis
3 Florence McDowell, *Other Days Around Me*, 1966
4 C. S. Lewis, *Surprised by Joy*, 1955

CHAPTER 13

1 Richard Jeffries, *Bevis: The Story of a Boy*, 1930
2 Kenneth Grahame, *The Golden Age*
3 Dylan Thomas, *Portrait of the Artist as a Young Dog*, 1940
4 Vladimir Nabokov, *Speak Memory*
5 Phyllis Bottome, *Search for a Soul*, 1947
6 Pearl S. Buck, *My Several Worlds*, 1954
7 Alison Uttley, *The Country Child*, 1932

180 *References*

8 Freya Stark, *Traveller's Prelude*, 1950
9 Freya Stark, *Traveller's Prelude*, 1950
10 Gwen Raverat, *Period Piece*
11 Verity Anderson, *The Northrepps Grandchildren*, 1968
12 Janet Hitchman, *The King of the Barbareens: The Autobiography of an Orphan*, 1960

CHAPTER 14

1 Anthea Holme and Peter Massie, *Children's Play. A Study of Needs and Opportunities, 1970*

CHAPTER 15

1 *The Plowden Report*
2 J. A. and T. H. Simms, *From Three to Thirteen*
3 W. D. Wall, *Child of Our Times*

CHAPTER 18

1 The Times Educational Supplement, 6 June 1969

Bibliography

The poorest man in the world is the man limited to his own experiences, the man who does not read.

DANIEL FADER, *Hooked on Books*

Allen, Lady Allen of Hurtwood, *Planning for Play*, Thames & Hudson, 1968

Aries, *Centuries of Childhood*, Cape, 1962

Axiline, V., *Dibs in Search of Self*, Houghton Mifflin, 1965

Baruch, Dorothy Walter, *Parents and Children Go to School*, Scott Foresman, 1939

Bloom, B. S., *Stability and Change in Human Characteristics*, Wiley 1964

Bowlby, J., *Maternal Care and Mental Health*, W.H.O., 1951; *Child Care and the Growth of Love*, Pelican, 1965

Boyce, E. R., *Play in the Infant School*, Methuen, 4th ed. 1951; *The First Year in School*, Nisbet, 1953

Bridges, K. M. B., *Social and Emotional Development of the Pre-School Child*, Kegan Paul, 1931

Burlingham, Dorothy and Freud, Anna, *Young Children in Wartime*, 1942; *Infants without Families,* Allen & Unwin, 1943

Cass, Joan E., *Literature and the Young Child*, Longmans, 1967

Chaloner, L., *Questions Children Ask*, Faber, 1952; *Feeling and Perception in Young Children*, Tavistock, 1963

Chesters, Gwendolen E., *The Mothering of Young Children*, Faber, 1953

Chukovsky, K., *From Two to Five*, University of California, 1966

Cleugh, M. F., *Psychology in the Service of the School*, Methuen, 1951

Cunningham, P. J., (ed.), *Nursery Nursing*, Faber, 1967

Cusden, P. E., *The English Nursery School*, Kegan Paul, 1938

Davidson, A. and Fay, J., *Phantasy in Childhood*, Routledge, 1952

Erikson, E. K., *Childhood and Society*, Hogarth, 1950; Pelican, 1965

Flügel, J. C., *The Psycho-Analytic Study of the Family*, Hogarth, 1921

Fraiberg, S. H., *The Magic Years*, Scribner's, 1959

Gabriel, J., *Children Growing Up*, U.L.P., 1968

Gardner, D. E. M., *The Education of Young Children*, Methuen, 1956

Gardner, D. E. M. and Cass, J. E., *The Role of the Teacher in the Infant and Nursery School*, Pergamon, 1965

Gardner, D. E. M., *Susan Isaacs. The First Biography*, Methuen, 1969

Gesell, A. and Ilg, F. L., *Infant and Child in the Culture of Today*, Harper, 1943

Hartley, R. E., Frank, L. K. and Goldenson, M., *Understanding Children's Play*, Routledge, 1952

Hegeler, F., *Choosing Toys for Children*, Tavistock, 1963

Hollanby, L., *Young Children Living and Learning*, Longmans, 1961

Holme, A. and Massie, P., *Children's Play, A Study of Needs and Purposes*, Michael Joseph, 1970

Hostler, P., *The Child's World*, Benn, 1953

Illingworth, R. S. and C. M., *Lessons from Childhood*, Livingstone, 1966

Isaacs, Susan, *The Nursery Years*, Routledge, 1929; *Intellectual Growth in Young Children*, Routledge, 1930; *Social Development in Young Children*, Routledge, 1933; *The Psychological Aspects of Child Development*, Evans, 2nd ed. 1949; *The Nature and Function of Phantasy-Developments in Psycho-Analysis*, Hogarth, 1952

Jackson, L. and Todd, K. M., *Child Treatment and the Therapy of Play*, Methuen, 1946

Jersild, A. T., *Child Psychology* (4th ed.), Staples

Kay, George and Cornelia, *Games and Play for the Sick Child*, Corgi, 1968

Kellmer Pringle, M. L., *Deprivation and Education*, Longmans, 1965

Klein, Melanie and Rivière, Joan, *Love, Hate and Reparation*, Hogarth, 1937

Klein, Melanie, *Envy and Gratitude, A Study of Unconscious*

Sources, Tavistock, 1957; *Our Adult World and its Roots in Infancy,* Tavistock, 1959

Laing, R. D., *The Divided Self,* Tavistock, 1959

Landreth, Catherine, *Education of the Young Child,* Wiley, 1944

Lowenfeld, M., *Play in Childhood,* Gollancz, 1935

Lynd, Sylvia, *English Children,* Collins, 1942

Marshall, Sybil, *An Experiment in Education,* C.U.P., 1963

May, Dorothy, *Children in the Nursery School,* U.L.P., 1963

Mellor, E., *Education through Experience in the Infant School,* Blackwell, 1950

Matterson, E. M., *Play with a Purpose for the Under Sevens,* Penguin, 1965

Millar, S., *The Psychology of Play,* Penguin, 1968

Miles, M., *Live and Learn,* Allen & Unwin, 1968

Mitchell, Marjorie (ed.), *The Child's Attitude to Death,* Barrie & Rockliffe, 1966

Molony, E. (ed.), *How to Form a Playgroup,* B.B.C., 1967

Morris, D., *The Naked Ape,* Cape, 1967

Newson, J. and E., *Patterns of Infant Care in an Urban Community,* Allen & Unwin, 1965; *Four Years Old in an Urban Community,* Allen & Unwin, 1968

Noble, E., *Play and the Sick Child,* Faber, 1967

Opie, Iona and Peter, *Children's Games in the Street and Play-ground,* O.U.P., 1969

Owens, Joan L., *Working with Children,* Bodley Head, 1962

Page, Hilary, *Playtime in the First Five Years,* Allen & Unwin, 1953

Peters, J., *Growing Up World,* Longmans, 1966

Piaget, J., *Play Dreams and Imitation in Childhood,* Routledge, 1951

Rayner, Claire, *A Parent's Guide to Sex Education,* Corgi, 1968

Read, H., *Education Through Art,* Faber, 1949

Ridgway, L. and Lawton, L., *Family Grouping in the Infant School,* Ward Lock, 1965

Robertson, J., *Young Children in Hospital,* Tavistock, 1958

Septima and Margett, *Child's Play,* Dent, 1970

Simms, J. A. and T. H., *From Three to Thirteen,* Longmans, 1969

Simpson and Alderson, *Creative Play in the Infant School,* Pitman, 1950

Tavistock Clinic Mini Corgi Books 1970, *Your 1 year old,* Dilys Daws; *Your 2 year old,* Dina Rosenbluth; *Your 3 year old,* Dina Rosenbluth; *Your 4 year old,* Elsie L. Osborne; *Your 5 year old,*

Elsie L. Osborne; *Your 6 year old,* Christopher Dare; *Your 7 year old,* Elsie L. Osborne; *Your 8 year old,* Edna O'Shaughnessy

Tustin, F., *A Group of Juniors,* Heinemann, 1951

Van der Eyken, Willem, *Pre-School Years* (Rev. ed.), Penguin, 1969

Wall, W. D., *Child of Our Time,* National Children's Home Convocation Lecture, 1959

Williams, J., *Psychology for Student Nurses,* Methuen, 1954

Willsher, Betty, *Call Me Person,* Pergamon, 1969

Winn, Marie and Porcher, Mary, *The Playgroup,* Souvenir Press, 1968

Winnicott, D. W., *The Child, The Family and the Outside World,* Penguin, 1964

Wolfheim, N., *Psychology in the Nursery School,* Duckworth, 1953

PAMPHLETS

The Nursery School Association, 89 Stamford Street, London SE1

'The Educational Value of the Nursery School' (Susan Isaacs)

'The Nursery School in Action' (B. Irene Grove)

'Starting a Community Nursery School' (A. Calverly)

National Froebel Foundation, 2 Manchester Square, London W1

'Scientific Interests in the Primary School' (G. Allen, V. Brown, H. Southam, E. Tuke)

National Society of Children's Nurseries, Montgomery Hall, Kennington, The Oval, London SE11

'Growth Through Play in the First Two Years' (B. Tudor-Hart)

The Save the Children Fund, 29 Queen Anne's Gate, London SW1

'Suggestions for Play Activities for Young Children' (D. E. May)

The National Association for Mental Health, 39 Queen Anne Street, London W1

'Children's Fears' (Ruth Thomas)

'Children's Jealousies' (Ruth Thomas)

The National Book League, 7, Albemarle Street, London W1

Book Lists and Book Exhibitions

The Pre-School Play Groups Association, 87a Borough High Street, London SE1

'Settling a Child into a Playgroup' (M. Sutton and G. Thorn)

'Playgroups at Work'

'Playgroups as Enrichment for the Under Fives'

REPORTS

Children and their Primary Schools. A Report of the Central
   Advisory Council for Education (England) *The Plowden Report*
   Vol. I and II, HMSO, 1967
Organization of Pre-Primary Education. XXIVth International Con-
   ference on Public Education, Geneva, 1961
*Report of the Consultative Committee on Infant and Nursery
   Schools,* HMSO, 1933
The State of Nursery Education, National Union of Teachers,
   Hamilton House, Mabledon Place, WCI, 1964
'Ministry of Housing and Local Government Circular 36/37'
The Developmental Progress of Infants and Young Children, M. D.
   Sheriden, HMSO, 1962

AUTOBIOGRAPHIES AND NOVELS
CONCERNED WITH CHILDREN

*The aim of every artist is to arrest motion, which is life, by artificial
means and hold it fixed so that a hundred years later, when a
stranger looks at it, it moves again, since it is life*
WILLIAM FAULKNER, *Paris Review,* 1958

Anderson, Verity, *The Northrepps Grandchildren,* Hodder &
   Stoughton, 1968
Baines, Frank, *Look Towards the Sea,* Quality Book Club, 1958.
Bottome, Phyllis, *Search for a Soul,* Faber, 1957
Buck, Pearl, *My Several Worlds,* John Day, 1954·
Church, Richard, *Over the Bridge,* Heinemann, 1955
Frank, Anne, *The Diary of a Young Girl,* Pan Books, 1954
Golding, William, *Lord of the Flies,* Faber, 1948
Gosse, Edmund, *Father and Son,* Heinemann, 1907
Grahame, Kenneth, *The Golden Age,* Lane, 1907
Hitchman, Janet, *The King of the Barbareens,* Putnam, 1960
Hughes, Richard, *High Wind in Jamaica,* Chatto & Windus, 1929
Jeffries, Richard, *Bevis, The Story of a Boy,* Dent, 1930
Lee, Laurie, *Cider with Rosie,* Hogarth Press, 1959
Lewis, C. S., *Surprised by Joy,* Geoffrey Bles, 1955
McDowell, Florence, *Other Days Around Me,* Longmans, 1966
Nabokov, Vladimir, *Speak Memory,* Weidenfeld & Nicholson, 1967

Raverat, Gwen, *Period Piece*, Faber, 1940
Stark, Freya, *Traveller's Prelude,* John Murray, 1950
Thomas, Dylan, *Portrait of the Artist as a Young Dog,* Guild Books, 1940
Uttley, Alison, *The Country Child*, Faber, 1931

Index